THE GIRLS OF THE GARDEN CLUB

A COMEDY IN THREE ACTS
BY JOHN PATRICK

DRAMATISTS
PLAY SERVICE
INC.

THE GIRLS OF THE GARDEN CLUB
Copyright © Renewed 2005, Bradley Wayne Strauman
and Steven Rehl, Executors of the Author's Estate
Copyright © 1980, John Patrick
Copyright © 1977, John Patrick
as an unpublished dramatic composition

All Rights Reserved

CAUTION: Professionals and amateurs are hereby warned that performance of THE GIRLS OF THE GARDEN CLUB is subject to payment of a royalty. It is fully protected under the copyright laws of the United States of America, and of all countries covered by the International Copyright Union (including the Dominion of Canada and the rest of the British Commonwealth), and of all countries covered by the Pan-American Copyright Convention, the Universal Copyright Convention, the Berne Convention, and of all countries with which the United States has reciprocal copyright relations. All rights, including without limitation professional/amateur stage rights, motion picture, recitation, lecturing, public reading, radio broadcasting, television, video or sound recording, all other forms of mechanical, electronic and digital reproduction, transmission and distribution, such as CD, DVD, the Internet, private and file-sharing networks, information storage and retrieval systems, photocopying, and the rights of translation into foreign languages are strictly reserved. Particular emphasis is placed upon the matter of readings, permission for which must be secured from the Author's agent in writing.

The English language amateur stage performance rights in the United States, its territories, possessions and Canada for THE GIRLS OF THE GARDEN CLUB are controlled exclusively by DRAMATISTS PLAY SERVICE, INC., 440 Park Avenue South, New York, NY 10016. No nonprofessional performance of the Play may be given without obtaining in advance the written permission of DRAMATISTS PLAY SERVICE, INC., and paying the requisite fee.

Inquiries concerning all other rights should be addressed to Dramatists Play Service, Inc., 440 Park Avenue South, New York, NY 10016.

SPECIAL NOTE
Anyone receiving permission to produce THE GIRLS OF THE GARDEN CLUB is required to give credit to the Author as sole and exclusive Author of the Play on the title page of all programs distributed in connection with performances of the Play and in all instances in which the title of the Play appears for purposes of advertising, publicizing or otherwise exploiting the Play and/or a production thereof. The name of the Author must appear on a separate line, in which no other name appears, immediately beneath the title and in size of type equal to 50% of the size of the largest, most prominent letter used for the title of the Play. No person, firm or entity may receive credit larger or more prominent than that accorded the Author.

THE GIRLS OF THE GARDEN CLUB was first presented by the Berea (Ohio) Summer Theatre, at Baldwin-Wallace College, in July, 1979. It was directed by Jack B. Winget; the scenic designer was Doug Hall; the costume designer was B. A. Kendig; and the lighting was designed by Kirk Bookman. The cast was as follows:

RHODA	Prudy Hock
VINCENT	Lou Morehead
CORA	Dorothy Canepari
LILLYBELLE	Sheila Mulligan Koster
MARIGOLD	Val Ciancutti
DORA	Alice Roddy Scott
BIRDIE	Alice Mobley
DEDE	Mary Ann Jamison
EVIE	Julie Smith
CLARA	Jean Onysko
DILLSON	Willard Franklin
ANGELICA	Shari Longworth
FRANCINE	Marge Meder
GINGER	Kathy Petro
RITA	Robin Anter
BERTHA	Diana Ferry
JUDI	Denise Leslie
MARGARET	Sally Suren
VERA	Joan Larter

And the Berea Garden Club

The action takes place in the living room of Vincent and Rhoda Greenleaf.

FOREWORD

Since this play calls for a very large cast, we suggest you entice the good ladies of your local Garden Club to become actors. This will not only fill your stage but also the *theater*, as *all* their relatives will want to see them "up there" acting! Good luck.

John Patrick

THE GIRLS OF THE GARDEN CLUB

ACT ONE

TIME: *The present.*
PLACE: *The living room of Rhoda Greenleaf, an average housewife of an average suburban village. She is personable and pleasant.*
The entrance is Upstage Left. There is a door to the kitchen Upstage Right. The stairs are next to the entrance door.
There are rafters from which various plants hang. With the profusion of potted ferns and flowers, the room resembles more a crowded solarium. Moving among the plants should be a hazard course.
There is a fireplace Stage Left with a plant beside it. A card table is set with cups and a coffee urn.
AT RISE: *Vincent Greenleaf, a balding man of great weight and weariness, sits in his undershirt in a deep chair reading the Sunday paper, with his feet up on an ottoman and a can of beer beside him.*
After a moment, Rhoda enters from the patio with a small ladder and a watering can. She looks around at her plants and places the ladder beside Vincent's chair.

RHODA. Vincent—you're sitting under my pteris multifida cristata. (*He glances up at his wife, blinks, then looks up at the hanging plant above him. He grunts, rises and crosses the room and sinks into another chair. Rhoda mounts her ladder and starts watering.*) You needn't grunt. If you'd take that Yale lock off your wallet and buy me a little greenhouse, I wouldn't have to keep my poor little plants huddled in here like poor little unwanted orphans. (*Her daughter Marigold, a pretty girl of 16, comes down the stairs in a robe, yawning.*) Well! I thought you were going to sleep forever, dear.
MARIGOLD. Oh, Mother—it's Sunday. (*Stops to kiss the top of her father's head.*) Good morning, Poppy-poop.

5

RHODA. *I'm* up. The sun is up. And my tulips are up. With your upbringing, *you* should be up.
MARIGOLD. (*Crosses toward kitchen.*) Yes, Mother, I'm sorry you're *uptight* and in an *uproar* because I'm not up to you, and your tulips, too. (*Exits into kitchen.*)
RHODA. (*Calls after her.*) There's some leftover biscuits you can toast for breakfast in the fridge behind the dog's dish, dear. (*She crosses with her ladder to Vincent.*) Vincent, you're under my tradescantia fluminensis variegata. (*He looks up at Rhoda, blinks again, then looks up at the plant above him and rises with a grunt. He crosses to another chair. Rhoda steps up on the ladder with her watering can.*) All the girls that belong to our Garden Club have greenhouses or at least a lean-to. I hardly have a pot to plant in. But I'm not going to nag. I have too much pride. Next winter, I'll just have to let my poor little helxine solieroli freeze to death in the snow. In case you're interested, helxine solieroli is better known as "Baby Tears." (*She continues watering. Marigold re-enters with a bowl of cereal. She slumps into a chair. She starts to light a cigarette.*) Marigold, it's bad enough that your father lets you smoke but *please* don't smoke next to my calathea makoyana. It wilts.
MARIGOLD. (*Moves over beside the card table.*) You know what you are, Mother? A flower-freak.
RHODA. Well, permit me to tell you something, Miss Sleeping Beauty. Civilization began with a flower. The first cave man to drop his club and pick a wild rose, became a human being. And if he smelled it, he became a poet.
MARIGOLD. Bring on the violins, professor.
RHODA. If you give love, you get love. You nurture a plant just as you'd nurture a person you love and the results are just as rewarding. I get the same nice feeling from looking at a dendrobrium I've raised that I get from looking at you, dear. Only a dendrobrium is easier to raise, and you don't have to send it to college.
MARIGOLD. Well, I wish to heck you hadn't named me Marigold.
RHODA. It's a lovely name. You were my little flower.
MARIGOLD. Not when jerks at school come up to you and say, "Can I smell you, Marigold?"
RHODA. Change it to "Goldie."
MARIGOLD. I will—if I ever become a hooker.
RHODA. That's no way to talk on Sunday. (*Marigold picks up a*

cup.) No—no! Don't touch those cups. I have that coffee set up for the Garden Club girls. They're coming over for a secret meeting.
MARIGOLD. (*Mockingly*.) Girls indeed. Old Mrs. Smithers must be crowding ninety.
RHODA. Crowding—but not there. She's barely eighty-eight. (*Glances at her daughter eating her cereal with eyes closed.*) Sweetheart—if you opened your eyes you could find the way to your mouth better. You're not going to look very attractive with a spoon up your nose.
MARIGOLD. Oh, Mother—I wish you'd practice "Nabb."
RHODA. Nabb? What's Nabb?
MARIGOLD. N.A. Double B. "No-Arguments-Before-Breakfast."
RHODA. Yes, dear. I'll practice "Nabb" when you show a little gumption.
MARIGOLD. Now, what's *that* supposed to mean?
RHODA. Gumption. G.U.M.P.T.—"Get Up Mornings Pleasant, Tolerant"—I.O.N—"Instead Of Nasty."
MARIGOLD. Where'd you read *that*?
RHODA. Reader's Digest. I've been waiting months to use it, thank you. (*The phone rings. Rhoda answers.*) Hello. Oh, hello Thelma. Oh! I'm so *sorry*. What are you doing for it? Well, the best cure I know is—do you have a pencil? Take a spoonful of boric acid in about a half a cup of warm water. Mix in a handful of manure—sterilized cow manure is best—
MARIGOLD. Please, Mother—I'm eating!
RHODA. But any good manure will do as long as it isn't fresh. (*Marigold flees into the kitchen.*) Pour a little on your African violets every two hours, dear, and they'll pick up like magic. Higgins Hardware has the best manure—they deliver once the cows have delivered. No trouble. Call me if anything else gets sick. (*She hangs up and calls toward the kitchen.*) Oh, Marigold, dear. Don't feed Socrates anything. The poor dog ate some of my cut-worm pellets and threw up his breakfast.
MARIGOLD. (*Offstage*.) Thanks, Mother—I'm about to do the same.
RHODA. (*Stands beside Vincent with her watering can.*) Sweetheart, you're sitting under my phoenix roebelenii. (*He shifts to another chair. Rhoda mounts her ladder to water.*) Patty Pringle has a greenhouse and her husband is a shoe clerk. Greta Grant has a greenhouse and her husband is only a truck driver. I should think

you'd be ashamed to go to Rotary. You're on the town council. What's the point of being in politics if you can't ask favors from the road commissioner—a little free sand and cement. The glass wouldn't cost much. You spent fifty dollars on chances when your Rotary Club raffled off that new Volkswagen Rabbit model for arteriosclerosis. But you wouldn't gamble fifty cents on me because I'm not a rabbit. Well, you won't hear any complaints from me. Even when I see a weeping fig weeping in the cold. (*Vince rises wearily and starts up the stairs.*) Sweetheart—Cora and some of the girls are coming over for coffee. If you come down again, please put on a shirt. I don't want them to think you haven't got a shirt because we can't afford a greenhouse. (*He goes on up silently. Rhoda looks up the stairs after him.*) You don't know it, Mr. Vincent Wellington Greenleaf, but you're in for a surprise. You're not the only politician in this family. (*The door chimes are heard.*) Oh, that must be Cora. (*Calls.*) Come in, Cora. (*The door opens. Instead of Cora, her son Dillson enters slovenly. He is 15, shaggy, gangling, and sloppily dressed. He wears rimless glasses and an air of boredom.*) Oh, it's you, Dillson.
DILLSON. Hi, Mrs. Greenleaf. Watering your weeds?
RHODA. No. I'm flying a kite. Isn't it obvious?
DILLSON. Oh. I get it. A sour-silly-sally.
RHODA. A what?
DILLSON. You know—a joke. A hanky-panky-pun.
RHODA. I'm sorry I asked. How's your Mother?
DILLSON. Grouchy.
RHODA. Is she coming over soon?
DILLSON. In a minute. She couldn't get Dad off the toilet. He sits there all Sunday morning reading the paper.
RHODA. I'm sorry I asked that, too.
DILLSON. (*Looks upstairs.*) Marigold awake?
RHODA. Partially. (*Indicates kitchen.*) She's eating breakfast.
DILLSON. I thought I'd come over and take her for a swim.
RHODA. Good. It might wake her up.
DILLSON. Do you mind if I use *your* pool?
RHODA. Not if you use your towel.
DILLSON. (*Starts for kitchen.*) I'm drip-dry. You know—a hippy-handy-dandy. (*He exits into kitchen with a smug cluck.*)
RHODA. (*Looks after him and sighs.*) There you have it in a nutshell. That boy explains why so many women turn from motherhood to horticulture. (*Vincent comes down the stairs. Rhoda stops him halfway.*)

Vincent! Put on a shirt. And your fly is open. (*He turns and goes back upstairs. The door chime is heard. Rhoda opens the door.*) Oh, come in Cora. (*Cora enters. She is an intelligent, forthright and affable mother in her middle forties, also.*) That darling boy of yours is already here, Cora.
CORA. Darling? You want him, you can have him.
RHODA. No, thank you. I have a daughter. I don't need a hippy-handy-dandy.
CORA. Pity.
RHODA. Well! How are you, dear, this bright and lovely morning?
CORA. Terrible.
RHODA. What's the matter?
CORA. I've got whitefly.
RHODA. Oh, that *is* terrible.
CORA. That's what I said. (*Sits.*)
RHODA. (*Puts her arm around her shoulder sympathetically.*) Where have you got it? On your gloxinia?
CORA. My hedera helix.
RHODA. Have you sprayed?
CORA. I've sprayed and prayed and sprayed again. Neither one does any good. They go right on breeding like bug degenerates.
RHODA. Have you tried malathion?
CORA. Herbert won't let me use it in the house. He says it smells like cat urine.
RHODA. Well, it does but you'll just have to choose between malathion, whitefly, cat urine or your husband.
CORA. I've raised that hedera helix from a little green cutting I stole from the cemetery.
RHODA. Bring it over here and I'll nurse it for you. Vincent doesn't mind cat urine since he went into politics.
CORA. You're a living saint, Rhoda. You should have been a nun.
RHODA. Well, heaven knows I'm on my knees enough, and if I ever get to heaven they'll never give me a harp. They'll give me a trowel. (*Vincent comes down the stairs, wearing a shirt this time.*)
CORA. Good morning, Vincent. (*Vincent raises one finger in acknowledgement and goes silently into kitchen.*) He's lost weight, hasn't he?
RHODA. Where?
CORA. Not very talkative before breakfast, is he?
RHODA. He's on strike.

CORA. From eating?
RHODA. No. He says he's not going to open his mouth in this house again until I shut mine about wanting a greenhouse.
CORA. Don't worry. Women outlive men. Shows you what spite can do.
RHODA. When he put in our swimming pool for Marigold, our taxes were raised. He says he's damned if he's going to have them raised again because of a *greenhouse* until the council raises his salary. (*Vincent returns carrying a can of beer.*)
CORA. Drinking beer this early, Vincent? (*He looks at the beer in his hand, then at his wristwatch and nods. He continues toward the stairs with a shrug.*)
RHODA. Don't leave your beer on my dresser, sweetheart—it leaves a ring. Too bad you never leave a ring with a diamond in it. (*He exits.*)
CORA. Well. Who else is coming this morning? You sounded urgent on the phone.
RHODA. Just a few of you girls I can trust. Dora and Evie—
CORA. Oh, not the Siamese twins!
RHODA. Why do you call them that?
CORA. Have you ever seen Evie without Dora? They're linked together with one brain. And that belongs to Evie.
RHODA. I thought you liked them.
CORA. I *do*. They're two of my *best* friends. Only I can't stand them for more than two minutes together.
RHODA. But Evie is still so pretty. To me, just her presence in a room decorates it.
CORA. So does wallpaper.
RHODA. And Dora wouldn't hurt a fly.
CORA. She's not smart enough. Do you know she'll buy *anything* if she can get trading stamps? She drives all the way over to West Maplewood because they give trading stamps with birdseed.
RHODA. I call that thrifty.
CORA. I call it stupid. Think of all the gas she wastes.
RHODA. Not if she gets gas trading stamps.
CORA. Do you know she bought three burial plots because they offered trading stamps?
RHODA. Well, that's looking ahead.
CORA. But there's just Dora and her husband. What's she going to do with an extra plot?
RHODA. Die happy, I guess.

CORA. And did you ever hear her express an opinion of her own? She's the original Mrs. Echo. She just repeats everything Evie says. I think her husband tells her when to go to the bathroom. Why did you invite *them?*
RHODA. I want girls in the Garden Club I can trust. I'll need all the help I can get. And they're indebted to me. I gave them each a cutting of begonia hispidulum last summer.
CORA. You didn't give me a hispidulum.
RHODA. But I gave you a socotrana.
CORA. Blackmailed for a begonia. Who do I kill for my socotrana?
RHODA. I'll tell you when the other girls get here. I have a plot.
CORA. So does Dora. And she's going to be buried in it. *(The door chimes ring.)*
RHODA. Well, anyhow, I'm glad you like them because that's probably them now. They're also linked together with a common vice—punctuality. *(She opens the door. Evie and Dora enter. Evie is a willowy blonde matron with good taste in clothes and makeup. Dora is her opposite—rather dowdy behind horn-rimmed glasses. She is most eager to be liked and uses a fixed smile for bait.)* Well, well, well. You girls look fine and fit this bright and early morning. *(Cora rises, waves and blows enthusiastic kisses.)*
CORA. Hi, Evie, dear. Wonderful to see you. Hello, Dora, sweetie.
RHODA. I'm so glad you could come.
EVIE. Well, actually, I didn't want to—I feel so awful.
DORA. She feels awful.
EVIE. My caladium died.
DORA. Her caladium died.
RHODA. Oh, how tragic! *(Pats her.)* I'll get you another one. There's a sale on at Neuffers Nursery and I need slug bait.
DORA. Do they give stamps?
RHODA. For driving that far, they should give you lunch and manure.
EVIE. No—a new caladium would be like adopting an orphan. It wouldn't be the same.
DORA. It wouldn't be the same.
EVIE. I guess I just haven't got a green thumb.
DORA. She just hasn't got a green thumb.
EVIE. I've lost so many of my flower friends lately, I'm beginning to feel cursed with blight.

DORA. Cursed with blight.
EVIE. I just may throw in the sponge and give up my hot-bed.
DORA. And she will.
CORA. Why don't you try Wandering Jew? Any fool can grow that.
EVIE. Oh, I wish you'd call it something else, Cora. That sounds *so* anti-Semitic.
RHODA. Say zebrina pendula—it's the same thing.
EVIE. (*Sweetly*.) But *is* it? It's like changing your name from Lipschitz to Lippencott. Who do you fool?
DORA. That's what *I* ask. Who do you fool?
CORA. The Anti-Defamation League.
RHODA. Well, anything's better than calling it a Wandering Lipschitz.
EVIE. Oh, Rhoda—you're awful! What if Reba Goldman heard that. She's my dearest friend. She'll think we mean her husband. He keeps a blonde in a condominium.
DORA. In a condominium.
EVIE. Who else is coming?
RHODA. Well, I asked old Mrs. Smithers because—
EVIE. Oh, not Birdie Smithers!
DORA. Not her!
RHODA. What's wrong with her! She loves our Garden Club and she gave fifty dollars last year to our "Save the Whistling Crane" drive. She's a dear.
EVIE. She's also deaf. After shouting at her for ten minutes, I'm as hoarse as a bullfrog.
DORA. She's as hoarse as a bullfrog.
EVIE. I can't help it. That's the way I am.
DORA. That's the way she is.
CORA. I don't mind her. (*Adds*.) After a few drinks.
RHODA. Well, I took care of her parakeet when she was in the hospital with hemorrhoids. She's been very grateful and I need her for my plan.
EVIE. What plan?
DORA. What plan?
RHODA. I'll tell you when the rest of the girls get here. (*The door chime rings*.) Well, that's one of them now. (*It rings again*.) No—it's old Mrs. Smithers. She can't hear her first ring so she always rings twice. (*Starts for door*.)
EVIE. I don't know why I don't trust my horoscope. It said I'd have a horrible day.

CORA. (*To Cora.*) That's what it said. Horrible.
RHODA. (*Opens door.*) Oh, what a surprise. It's *you*, Mrs. Smithers. Did you walk over? (*Birdie Smithers enters. She looks like a gnome and is equally quixotic. She wears an ancient hat over her ancient face and her glasses are balanced on the tip of her nose. Her clothes are early Salvation Army. Rhoda kisses her.*)
GIRLS. (*Together.*) Hello, Birdie, dear. (*She ignores the chorus as she looks up, slack-jawed, at Rhoda.*)
BIRDIE. (*Shouts.*) What'd you say?
RHODA. (*Raises her voice.*) I said did you walk over?
BIRDIE. Wait'll I tune you in. (*Adjusts her hearing-aid.*) Now. What'd you say?
RHODA. (*Yells.*) I said—did you walk over?
BIRDIE. (*Softly.*) No. I skated. What are you whispering for?
RHODA. Sorry. I've got a cold.
BIRDIE. Then you shouldn't have kissed me. (*Looks over at the girls.*) Who's here? A lot of old cackling hens?
RHODA. Just your friends.
CORA. Nice to see you, Birdie.
EVIE. Nice to see you, Birdie.
DORA. Nice to see you, Birdie.
BIRDIE. (*To Rhoda.*) What'd they say?
GIRLS. (*Shout together.*) Nice to see you, Birdie.
RHODA. Here—let me have that. (*Takes her umbrella.*) Why do you always carry an umbrella, Birdie? Afraid of rain?
BIRDIE. No—afraid of dogs.
RHODA. Well, here—sit down and be comfortable.
BIRDIE. I can't be comfortable till my hemorrhoids heal. Got an innertube I can sit on?
RHODA. This chair has a pillow.
BIRDIE. (*Stares at chair.*) Don't you have a rocker?
RHODA. I'll have one for you next time.
BIRDIE. There may not be a next time. (*Sits.*) I'm already twenty-five years past Medicare.
RHODA. You're lucky.
BIRDIE. Yep. The government paid for my hemorrhoids—the bastards.
RHODA. (*Sits beside her.*) Well, tell us what you've been up to.
BIRDIE. Been up to Boston.
RHODA. Oh, I didn't know that.
BIRDIE. What'd you say?
RHODA. (*Louder.*) I said I didn't know that.

BIRDIE. I just told you.
CORA. Did you have a good time?
BIRDIE. You're not supposed to have a good time at a funeral. (*Adds.*) Not in Boston.
RHODA. Oh, did somebody die?
BIRDIE. They thought so—so they buried him. It was hard to tell with Otis. (*Cackles with pleasure.*)
CORA. Anyone close?
BIRDIE. Well, I wouldn't consider Boston close. Half-brother. Half-wit. Half-ass. Never did like him. Democrat.
RHODA. Well, at least you won't have to go again.
BIRDIE. Not unless they dig him up and bury him again.
RHODA. Well, that's hardly likely.
BIRDIE. I don't know. He never could stay in one place.
EVIE. Could we change the subject from dying and hemorrhoids? Was it humid up in Boston?
DORA. Was it humid?
BIRDIE. It's always humid in Boston. Too many people breathing up there.
EVIE. Did you like it when you lived in Boston?
BIRDIE. I didn't know you were *supposed* to *like* it. You live with it. Like being born cross-eyed.
CORA. This is getting nowhere fast. Rhoda—can you tell us what we're here for now?
RHODA. Wait'll Dede gets here.
BIRDIE. Who?
RHODA. Dede Lovewell. Also—
BIRDIE. *She's* coming?
RHODA. Yes. Why?
BIRDIE. (*Rises.*) *I'm* going.
RHODA. Wait! Don't you like her?
BIRDIE. Love her. My dearest friend. Gave me a potted Fluffy Ruffle. But she squeals. Hurts me eardrums.
EVIE. Birdie's right. Dede's a squealer. I went to the Flower Show with her. She screamed over every exhibit. She can start dogs barking a mile away.
DORA. A mile away.
RHODA. She's enthusiastic. I think enthusiasm can be rewarding.
BIRDIE. If you're a prostitute—it pays big.
RHODA. Please stay, Birdie. You can tune her out. (*Birdie sits again—carefully.*)

CORA. The only thing I've got against Dede—and I love her—is—she talks to flowers.
EVIE. Some people think it helps.
DORA. Some people.
RHODA. Well, personally, I'd feel foolish saying "Hello, Gladys" to a gladiola.
CORA. Dede reacts more passionately to a *night*-blooming cereus than she does to her husband.
BIRDIE. Maybe that's because his own cereus doesn't bloom at night anymore.
EVIE. I'll make a bet with anyone here that she screams over something before anyone can say chlorophytum comosum vittatum. That's a spider plant.
DORA. That's a spider plant.
CORA. What'd you have in mind?
EVIE. My Crown of Thorns against your fishtail palm.
CORA. Make it a Moses in the Cradle and you've got a deal. (*There is a knock on the door.*)
RHODA. (*Starts for door.*) That Dede. She always knocks. She says a bell is artificial—as bad as artificial flowers.
CORA. (*To Evie.*) I think I should warn you, Evie—my Crown of Thorns has spider mite.
EVIE. That's alright—my fishtail has aphids.
DORA. And it does. Aphids.
RHODA. (*Opens door.*) Dede! We were just talking about you. (*Dede Lovewell enters. She is tall, thin, and fluttery. She bats her eyelashes a lot. She wears a rose and a beatific smile.*)
DEDE. Am I late? (*She glances at the plant beside the fireplace, points and screams.*) Oh! Oh! (*She flutters over to the plant.*)
CORA. There goes my Moses in the Cradle.
DEDE. Oh—your *beautiful* Polypody! *However* did you *do* it!
RHODA. Love and water.
DEDE. I've never *seen* such a *healthy* plant. It's *catastrophic!*
RHODA. No—just a Polypody.
DEDE. Look how it stands up—so brave and proud.
RHODA. Just goes to show what a little manure will do. (*Dede sees another plant and squeals. She dashes over to it.*)
DEDE. Oh! Oh—I'm going to *die*.
BIRDIE. I *hope* not. I've just been to *one* funeral.
DEDE. I *don't* believe it! Who else could grow a gynura like that.

Who—who—who! Touch me, Rhoda—give me some of your magic.
RHODA. I'll give you some of my manure.
DEDE. (*Starts across the room, stopping at each plant.*) Hi, Hyacinth. (*To next plant.*) Hello, Holly. (*To next plant.*) Hello, Fern. (*Reaches Cora.*) Hello, Cora. Hello, all you'all. Did you *see* Rhoda's Polypody? Isn't it splendiferous!
BIRDIE. Oh, sit down, Dede, before you wet your pantyhose.
DEDE. Birdie! That's no way to talk in front of flowers.
CORA. I hope you mean me.
RHODA. Do you really think it helps to talk to flowers, Dede?
DEDE. I *know* it does. Last year my retroflexa tulips were so depressed by the weather they wouldn't lift their little heads. (*She demonstrates with limp wrists and hanging head.*) After one week of telling them how much I loved them—do you know what happened?
BIRDIE. They died.
DEDE. No! They lifted their heads to the sun— (*She demonstrates.*) —and actually smiled. (*She smiles. There is a moment of silent doubt.*)
BIRDIE. Do that again.
DEDE. Well, it's true. They're very sensitive.
BIRDIE. So am I. I've just had hemorrhoids.
RHODA. Thank you, girls, for coming over. You see, I need your help. I've reached a crisis in my life.
CORA. Menopause?
BIRDIE. That's no crisis. When you're married to a sex maniac, it's a blessing.
CORA. Were *you*? How do *you* know?
BIRDIE. Married two of 'em. Kept me *young*. Killed *them*.
DEDE. (*To a plant.*) Don't listen, Myrtle.
RHODA. As you probably know, I want a greenhouse and Vincent won't buy me one.
EVIE. I consider that mental cruelty.
DORA. And mean, too.
RHODA. But he committed himself in our last argument. (*Adds.*) In a way.
DEDE. What do you mean—in a way?
RHODA. Well, I pointed out to him that even the White House had a greenhouse. And he said—when you're President, you can have a greenhouse. So I've decided to run for President.

CORA. Oh, Rhoda, no *woman* could be elected President of this country. Not yet.
BIRDIE. And you'll get hemorrhoids waiting.
RHODA. I don't mean the United States,— (*Loftily.*) I mean—*The Garden Club!* Our own Upper South Ho-Ho-Kus Little Lake Garden Club!
BIRDIE. You haven't got a chance in a pig's ass.
DEDE. Birdie! If you continue to use foul language, I'm going to move all these innocent plants out of this room into the sun.
DORA. And she will. That's the way she is.
CORA. Rhoda, Lillybelle Lamont has been President ever since she moved here. You can't win against her.
RHODA. I can if you'll help me. Nobody really likes her.
CORA. They like the parties she gives.
DEDE. I go because where else will you get fresh caviar? But I do wish she wouldn't use French phrases all the time. She makes me feel so stupid.
DORA. She makes her feel stupid.
DEDE. Do you think she *really* went to school in France?
BIRDIE. Probably worked in a French restaurant. Any sophisticated woman of taste and breeding need know only one word in French.
CORA. Which is?
BIRDIE. Merde.
EVIE. What does it mean?
DORA. In English.
BIRDIE. Bullshit.
EVIE. I knew I shouldn't have asked.
DORA. And she shouldn't have.
RHODA. Well, in spite of her two gardeners, two maids, two Bentleys, two face lifts, and too much money, I'm going to run against her.
BIRDIE. You haven't got a chance in a—
DEDE. Don't say it!
CORA. You'll never get enough votes, Rhoda.
RHODA. That's where you come in. I want you all to help solicit support to get the rules for election changed. I want you to recommend that whoever wins first prize at the Flower Show, will automatically become our next President. *That* gives me a chance.
CORA. What makes you think you can win first prize? (*Rhoda takes two bulbs out of a box and holds them up.*)

RHODA. Do you know what these are?
BIRDIE. They look like a couple of some old billy goat's dried testicles.
DEDE. Birdie! Pomona is going to strike you dead. (*To the others.*) Pomona's the Greek goddess of fruit trees.
DORA. Greek.
RHODA. These are the only two bulbs of their kind in this country. My cousin sent them to me. She's a nun in Burma.
BIRDIE. (*Shouts.*) What'd she say?
CORA. (*Shouts.*) Her cousin's a nun in Burma.
BIRDIE. (*Shouts back.*) *What's* a nun doing with testicles?
CORA. (*Shouts.*) Ask the Pope.
RHODA. These bulbs were taken from the King's own Royal Gardens. They're called Naga-Naga. That means Sleeping Virgin in Urdu. My cousin's a Naga nun.
BIRDIE. A Naga nun? Must live in an oyster cloister.
RHODA. (*Shows a snapshot.*) Here's a picture of my cousin holding a Sleeping Virgin in bloom.
EVIE. It's fabulous!
DORA. Fabulous.
DEDE. I don't *believe* it. Look at the flowers!
CORA. (*Passes photo on to Birdie.*) Fascinating. Did you ever see anything like this before?
BIRDIE. Never. *That's* your cousin? Short isn't she? First time I ever saw a midget nun.
CORA. I mean the plant. Don't you agree she could win first prize?
BIRDIE. The plant could. That nun couldn't.
RHODA. The blossom is the Virgin's awakening.
BIRDIE. What wakes her?
RHODA. The sun!
BIRDIE. Whose son?
DEDE. Birdie—you know why you're such a good gardener? You love dirt.
BIRDIE. Why not? God made the first man out of dirt. What was good enough for God is good enough for me. Dirt!
RHODA. Now you see why I'm so confident. Besides, the best gardener *should* be President. Lillybelle doesn't know anything about her plants. Her gardener has to tell her.
CORA. How do you know?
RHODA. I tested her.

EVIE. You did?
DORA. Did you?
EVIE. How?
DORA. How?
RHODA. I asked her if she planted her gluteus in the sun or in the shade.
CORA. Well, *I* don't know. Where *do* you plant it?
RHODA. On a toilet seat. Your gluteus is your behind.
BIRDIE. (*Shouts.*) What'd she say?
EVIE. (*Shouts back.*) She said your gluteus is your buttocks.
DORA. Your behind.
BIRDIE. Imagine that! Had one all these years and didn't know what to call it.
DEDE. She might have misunderstood what you said.
RHODA. Not a chance. Then I asked her if she grew any "Creeping Scrofula."
CORA. Does she?
RHODA. Oh, come on, Cora. Scrofula is a skin disease.
EVIE. I can't believe it.
DORA. She can't. She said so.
RHODA. You won't believe this either. I asked, quite seriously, if she had any Mountain Urinals and she said she'd ordered a dozen plants.
EVIE. Oh, you were naughty to do that, Rhoda. (*Waves a finger.*)
DORA. Naughty. (*Waves a finger.*)
RHODA. She doesn't know her aspidistra from a hole in the ground.
CORA. Maybe. But if she finds out you're out to change the rules—she's going to rule you out in a hurry.
DEDE. I hate dissension. That's what I love about flowers. They never fight.
EVIE. Well, tell us in so many words what you expect *us* to do.
DORA. In so many words.
RHODA. Wait 'till Clara gets here.
ALL. (*Together.*) Who!
RHODA. Clara Kimbal.
ALL. (*Together.*) *Clara Kimbal!*
RHODA. Now, you've all told me you think she's wonderful.
CORA. She is—as club secretary.
EVIE. But I'd hate to be trapped in an elevator with her. I'd prefer a Great Dane.

DORA. That's a dog.
DEDE. She doesn't really like flowers. She only grows mint and parsley in her window.
RHODA. Now what have you got against poor Clara?
CORA. Nothing. Absolutely nothing. Except she's dreary, dismal, dull, stern, strict, stubborn, opinionated and constipated. Outside of that, I worship the ground she walks on.
DEDE. She's always *correcting* me.
EVIE. Who needs that?
DORA. Nobody.
CORA. She's still an old maid schoolteacher at heart.
BIRDIE. (*Shouts.*) There's nothing wrong with Clara that a good romp in the hay wouldn't cure.
DEDE. Birdie—I'm not going to sit next to you.
CORA. The trouble with Clara is, she thinks a contradiction is a contribution to conversation. (*The door chime is heard. Rhoda starts for the door.*)
RHODA. Well, that's Clara now. Be nice to her. She's so good at organizing. And she doesn't have much in life to love.
CORA. Except her mint and parsley. I'll bet the *first* thing she'll do is correct one of us.
RHODA. (*Opens door.*) Clara, dear—we were just talking about you. Were your ears burning?
CLARA. (*Entering.*) That's an accepted but invalid fallacy. Your ears would only burn if you *heard* what was said. Good morning, ladies.
CORA. I told you.
EVIE. Hello, Clara, dear.
DORA. Hello, Clara, dear.
DEDE. Greetings, Clara.
BIRDIE. Mornin', Clara.
CORA. Hi, Clara, you're late.
CLARA. No. I'm early.
CORA. (*Looks at clock.*) It's ten-thirty isn't it?
CLARA. (*Looks at her watch.*) No—it's ten twenty-nine.
CORA. (*Smiles.*) Oh, well, it's not a matter of life or death, dear.
CLARA. It could be if your life depended on a split-second decision.
CORA. I didn't mean to start an argument, honey.
CLARA. Stating a fact is not necessarily an argument, Cora.
CORA. I'm sorry I said anything, Sweetie. Now—does that make you happy?

CLARA. Well, I'd hardly equate happiness with accuracy.
CORA. All right, Clara, I wish I were dead.
CLARA. Nor is despair an incentive to learning.
CORA. Oh, make no mistake, I've learned something. To keep my big mouth shut.
CLARA. It so happens I chose this watch with great caution.
DORA. I got mine with trading stamps.
CLARA. Well, may I inquire what I'm here for? There must be a reason or I wouldn't be asked.
RHODA. There is. I need your help. Your support. Frankly, if I can be elected Garden Club President, I can make Vincent give me a greenhouse.
CLARA. By "make" do you mean "force"?
RHODA. It's the same thing.
CLARA. Not quite. "Make" is to create or construct. "Force" is to exert power.
RHODA. Very well, I will exert *power* to *make* him construct a greenhouse.
BIRDIE. Wake me up when you get to the point.
CLARA. But Lillybelle Lamont is always voted in. Year after year.
RHODA. That's just the point. I want all my friends to campaign to have the rules changed.
CORA. She wants the next President to be whoever wins first prize at the Flower Show.
CLARA. But isn't that a presumption that presupposes that Rhoda can win?
BIRDIE. Show her your testicles, Rhoda.
RHODA. (*Holds up bulbs.*) I have two of the rarest bulbs in the world here. They'll blossom in time for this year's Flower Show.
CLARA. What are they called?
BIRDIE. You'll be sorry you asked.
RHODA. Sleeping Virgins.
CLARA. What horticultural vulgarity!
RHODA. And they're only grown in the King's Garden in Burma.
CORA. Her cousin is a Naga nun.
BIRDIE. A midget. Only comes up to your belly button.
RHODA. Anyhow, I've worked out a plan.
CLARA. Do you mean plan or strategem?
RHODA. (*A little annoyed.*) Oh, what's the difference?
CLARA. A plan is a drawing or diagram to clarify projected proposals. A strategem is a scheme for achieving some deceptive purpose.

CORA. Clara—I've got a great idea. Why don't you change your name from Clara Kimbal to "Clarification"?
CLARA. (*Smiles sweetly.*) Because I deplore the obvious, dear.
RHODA. Cora's just joking. Let's not quibble. I want to drop this bombshell at the next meeting of the whole Garden Club, which will be held here on Sunday the twenty-third.
CLARA. Oh, dear. That's the day Joan of Arc was burned at the stake.
RHODA. And here's the plan—or strategem. After Lillybelle calls the meeting to order and the official business is over, Dede—I want you to go to the mantelpiece there and pick up a book that I'll leave. Then give one of your famous shrieks to attract attention.
CORA. The one that wakes sleeping dogs?
RHODA. Then you say, "Girls! Girls! I want to recommend this wonderful book called 'Do's and Don't's for Dahlias.' "
DEDE. Will you give me a signal when?
RHODA. Yes. I'll say, "Does anybody want any cranberry juice?" That'll be your cue.
EVIE. "Does anybody want any cranberry juice?" I'll try to remember.
DORA. She'll try to remember.
RHODA. Then, Cora, when we have everyone's attention, you can say, "Girls! Girls! I want to take this opportunity to recommend a change in the rules this year."
CORA. Let me get this straight. *Her* cue is "cranberry juice" and mine is "Do's and Don't's."
BIRDIE. This sounds like a damned silly Democratic Convention.
RHODA. Then Clara, as club secretary, will say, "Does anybody second the motion" before anyone can object.
DEDE. May I suggest Dora to second it?
CORA. Try and stop her.
CLARA. No. That's wrong, Cora.
CORA. You think it would be a mistake?
CLARA. No—it's wrong grammatically. You don't say "try *and*." You say "try *to*."
CORA. "And" or "to," Dora is a born seconder, second to none.
DEDE. Could we go over it once. I don't want to make a mistake.
RHODA. All right. You'll be over by the fireplace, Dede. I'll be over here to give you your cue.
DEDE. (*She goes to the fireplace and takes up her position.*) I feel like Lauren Bacall.

CORA. You don't look like her, dear.
RHODA. Are you ready for your line?
DEDE. I'm ready.
RHODA. (*Clears her throat.*) "Does anybody here want any cranberry juice?" (*Vincent comes down the stairs.*) Wait a minute. (*He crosses to the kitchen in silence.*)
CLARA. Nice day, Vincent. For June. Rained five inches last year. Six the year before. Remember? (*He shakes his head and goes into the kitchen.*)
BIRDIE. He's lost weight, hasn't he?
CLARA. And his memory.
RHODA. No—but he's lost his argument with *me*—if you'll help. (*Glances toward kitchen.*) We can go ahead. He's probably gone out to the pool. He loves to watch Marigold swim.
DEDE. I'm ready. Will you give me my cue again?
RHODA. (*Clears her throat again.*) "Does anyone here want any cranberry juice?" (*Vincent returns with a can of beer.*) Wait! (*They wait in silence as Vincent goes back up the stairs.*)
BIRDIE. What does he do—sit on the can with a can?
DEDE. Will you say your line once more, Rhoda? I don't want to forget it.
RHODA. All right—here we go again. (*Thru clenched teeth.*) Does anyone here want any cranberry juice!
EVIE. (*Squeals. And then in an "acting voice."*) Oh! Girls—girls! I want to recommend this wonderful book called— (*She picks up the book—and stops.*)
RHODA. Well, what's the matter, Evie!
EVIE. This isn't "Do's and Don't's." (*Holds it up.*) It's "Fun with Ferns."
DORA. And it is.
RHODA. It doesn't matter! At the meeting it'll be "Do's and Don't's." I'll see to that.
EVIE. Well, I didn't know.
DORA. She didn't know.
RHODA. One more time. "*Does anyone here want any cranberry juice!*"
EVIE. (*Squeals.*) Oh! Girls! Girls! I want to recommend this *wonderful* book called "Do's and Don't's for Dahlias."
CORA. (*Climbs up on ladder.*) Girls! Girls—now that I've got your attention—I want to recommend— (*She stops. The door bell chimes.*) There's someone at the door.
RHODA. I wonder what for?

BIRDIE. Cranberry juice, probably.
RHODA. I didn't invite anyone else. (*Starts for door.*)
CORA. It may be a telegram.
DEDE. Maybe somebody died!
BIRDIE. Maybe they dug up Otis.
RHODA. (*Opens door.*) Oh! Lillybelle.
CORA. (*On the ladder.*) The place is bugged.
RHODA. (*Holds door open wider.*) What a surprise. Come in. (*She steps aside and Lillybelle Lamont enters. She is richly attired—almost flamboyantly. She is languid, exudes confidence, money and sugar-coated cunning.*)
LILLYBELLE. I was just driving by and— (*Sees the others.*) Evie! "Ma chéri!" (*Holds out her arms and crosses to embrace her. Turns to Dora.*) Dora—"Bonjour, bonjour!" (*Sees Cora on ladder.*) Cora—whatever are you doing up there?
CORA. Rehearsing Macbeth. (*Quotes.*) "Out, damned spot!" (*Climbs down and is embraced.*)
LILLYBELLE. Ma bébé!—how do you do it! That wonderful complexion. "Très formidable." What *do* you use?
CORA. Chicken fat.
LILLYBELLE. Oh, I *love* your sense of humor. So "très bien." (*Crosses to Birdie.*) Birdie—you get younger everytime I see you. "Comment allez-vous, Madame?" (*She curtseys.*)
BIRDIE. What are you doing?
LILLYBELLE. A lady always curtseys before royalty.
BIRDIE. She does?
LILLYBELLE. Oh, mais oui! It's proper. Oui, oui!
BIRDIE. Well, if you're a lady, I guess it *is* proper to squat if you're going to wee-wee.
LILLYBELLE. Birdie! At your age! You really shouldn't indulge in such liberties.
BIRDIE. At my age it's the only liberty left.
LILLYBELLE. Méchant! Méchant! (*To Rhoda.*) Am I interrupting anything? I saw your cars parked in front and wondered if I'd forgotten a meeting.
RHODA. No—we're all neighbors and just got together for coffee.
LILLYBELLE. Oh, well, I won't intrude. "Excusez-moi." (*Starts for door.*)
RHODA. No—no. Stay. Would you like a cup of coffee?
LILLYBELLE. Well, I always say you make the best coffee in town. "Très formidable."

BIRDIE. Saying that all the time must get damned tiresome. (*Rhoda goes to coffee table.*)
LILLYBELLE. Oh Birdie, you minx! "Méchant." (*Sits beside her.*) I just hope I have your wit when I'm your age.
BIRDIE. It won't be easy.
LILLYBELLE. "Ma chéri," I'm glad I ran into you. I've been planning to invite you to lunch for weeks.
BIRDIE. Then you better hurry. I'll be eighty-eight the thirtieth of May. That's Memorial Day, when they honor the dead.
CLARA. (*Distressed.*) Oh, dear. Why don't you *change* your birth date?
BIRDIE. You mean go back to my mother's womb! It's too long a trip.
CLARA. No. But the thirtieth of May was the day Mary, Queen of Scots had her head cut off.
BIRDIE. You may not believe this—but I wasn't there.
LILLYBELLE. Tell me, "Chéri," what have you been up to?
BIRDIE. Been up to Boston.
LILLYBELLE. Did you fly?
BIRDIE. No. I skated.
LILLYBELLE. (*Laughs gaily.*) Oh, you "ange." Let me take you to lunch tomorrow at my golf club.
BIRDIE. I haven't played golf since Lincoln was shot.
LILLYBELLE. But you have to eat. I'll have the chef fix up something special for you. What do you like best?
BIRDIE. Yogurt.
LILLYBELLE. Any particular flavor?
BIRDIE. Turnip.
LILLYBELLE. Your wish is my command. "Vou êtes un ange." (*Rhoda hands her a cup of coffee.*) Merci, Rhoda, merci. (*Looks into cup.*) Oh, dear. You put cream in it. I thought you remembered.
RHODA. Sorry. I forgot. (*Takes cup back.*) I'll get you another.
LILLYBELLE. No—no—don't bother. I'll do without.
RHODA. No trouble.
LILLYBELLE. (*Turns to Cora.*) Well, Cora—what's new in your life?
CORA. Whitefly.
LILLYBELLE. What are you spraying with?
CORA. Cat urine.
LILLYBELLE. What?
CORA. Malathion.
LILLYBELLE. Well, if it doesn't work, I'll send my handsome

young gardener over—"très formidable." You can have him anytime. Horticulturally, I mean.
CORA. I may take you up on that. Horticulturally.
LILLYBELLE. (*Crosses to Evie and takes her hand.*) Evie, "chéri," where did you get that devine bracelet? "Tres magnifique!"
EVIE. Woolworth's.
LILLYBELLE. Oh, you're jesting. It looks like real jade. "Authentique."
EVIE. It's only glass.
DORA. Plain glass.
RHODA. (*Returns with coffee.*) Would you like a brownie with it?
LILLYBELLE. Did you put sugar in, dear?
RHODA. (*Proudly.*) Yes. At least I remembered *that*.
LILLYBELLE. Oh, but I'm on a diet now. Oh, I should have told you. May I have it black, dear? Am I putting you to a lot of trouble?
RHODA. Not at all. I need the exercise. (*Rhoda takes cup back. Lillybelle turns to Evie.*)
LILLYBELLE. Could I ask an outrageous favor of you, Evie? Because you have so much better taste than I have.
EVIE. Oh, I wouldn't say that.
DORA. She wouldn't say that.
LILLYBELLE. Will you trade bracelets with me? "S'il vou plaît."
EVIE. I'd feel I was cheating you.
DORA. She'd feel she was cheating you.
LILLYBELLE. "Absurdité." Part of its value would be it once belonged to *you*.
EVIE. Well, if you say.
DORA. If you say. (*They trade bracelets as Rhoda returns with another cup of coffee.*)
RHODA. See if this is all right.
LILLYBELLE. (*Sips it.*) It's heaven! You know, Rhoda, what I really stopped in for was to see that darling daughter of yours. Is she here?
RHODA. Yes. I'll get her. (*She goes out.*)
LILLYBELLE. Isn't Rhoda an angel? Never complains. And she has so much to complain about.
BIRDIE. Yep. Her friends.
LILLYBELLE. And they're loyal and legion. Including me. But I feel so sorry for her. She wants a greenhouse so badly but poor Vincent hasn't the money.
CORA. How do you know that?

LILLYBELLE. He gambles, you know.
EVIE. He does?
DORA. Does he?
LILLYBELLE. Didn't you know? I'm told he gambled *hundreds* trying to win that Rabbit at Rotary.
BIRDIE. *(Shouts.)* A rabbit?
CLARA. *(Shouts to Birdie.)* It's a car.
BIRDIE. Oh. Thought she meant a bunny.
LILLYBELLE. And look at this. *(Holds up cup.)* A chipped cup. Doesn't it break your heart? "C'est triste!"
BIRDIE. Whatever the hell *that* means. *(Rhoda returns with Marigold and Dillson, both in their bathing suits.)*
MARIGOLD. Oh, hello, Mrs. Lamont.
DILLSON. Hi, Mrs. Lamont.
LILLYBELLE. "Mon dieu." Look at them. Was anyone really ever sixteen? They're little buds about to blossom.
DILLSON. Buddy—that's me.
LILLYBELLE. Oh, how I envy you, Cora—having such a witty son.
CORA. You want him—take him. I'll even throw in a potted petunia.
LILLYBELLE. No, but I'd like to help him blossom. Dillson, what are you doing?
DILLSON. Like when?
LILLYBELLE. I mean for spending money.
DILLSON. Praying.
LILLYBELLE. Would you like to assist me with my gardening?
DILLSON. For money?
LILLYBELLE. Naturally.
DILLSON. Then the answer is—naturally.
LILLYBELLE. And Marigold, I desperately need someone to help me with letters and shopping. Would you consider working with me? Naturally, I pay you. Would you like that, "Ma petite chéri?"
MARIGOLD. Like Dillson says—naturally.
CLARA. *As* Dillson says—not "like" he says. Watch your grammar, dear.
MARIGOLD. *I* thank you, Mrs. Lamont. My Father thanks you. My Mother thanks you. And my "grammar" thanks you.
DILLSON. Me, too. You're a real dilly-dandy-dolly, Mrs. Lamont. *(They dash out.)*
LILLYBELLE. Oh, dear. The summer of youth is so soon gone.

"C'est triste—c'est triste." (*Rises.*) Well, I must be going now. I don't want to intrude. "Merci beaucoup," Rhoda, for your divine coffee.
EVIE. Oh, Lillybelle, before you go, you *must* see Rhoda's Polypody.
DORA. Her Polypody.
LILLYBELLE. Of course, I adore Polypodys. I've several, you know. (*Goes to hanging basket.*) Isn't it lovely? So, so—"Très magnifique."
RHODA. That's my Wandering Jew, Lillybelle. The Polypody is by the fireplace.
LILLYBELLE. I know—I know. I'm getting to it. (*Continues to fireplace.*) Well, all I can say, Rhoda, is—you've proved it again.
RHODA. Yes—I think I have, dear.
CORA. Evie thinks that since Reba Goldman joined the club, we shouldn't say Wandering Jew. She's very sensitive about her husband and you-know-who.
LILLYBELLE. And she's so right. We mustn't hurt Reba. But what could we call it?
CORA. How about Wandering Armenian? We don't have any Armenians.
RHODA. We've already vetoed "Wandering Lipschitz."
LILLYBELLE. Of *course!* Well, I'll see what I can come up with. (*Blows kisses.*) "Au revior à tous. On ne voudrait pas appeler une jolie plante 'Wandering Lipschitz.' " (*She goes out.*)
BIRDIE. (*Shouts.*) What the hell was that all about?
CORA. (*Shouts back.*) Who knows!
RHODA. I'd like to know what she really came over here for. Buttering up everybody. She wants something. I wish I knew what.
BIRDIE. You want *me* to tell you?
RHODA. I certainly do.
BIRDIE. Put your hands over your ears, Evie. (*To Rhoda.*) She wants to be re-elected so everyone will still kiss her—pardon my French—kiss her gluteus—better known as her Royal ass.

CURTAIN

ACT TWO

PLACE: *The same.*
TIME: *Several weeks later.*
AT RISE: *Many chairs have been arranged in a semicircle facing the audience with a cardtable in the Center* U. *There are chairs behind the chairs facing, forming a second row. Vincent, in undershirt, sits in an extra chair reading his paper.*
Rhoda, dressed for the club's official meeting, enters from the kitchen with a glass and water pitcher which she places on the cardtable U. *She tests the gavel on the table. She then crosses down to the coffee table and picks out "Do's and Don'ts" from the shelf of the coffee table. She takes it to the mantel and puts it pointedly in place. She then surveys the room and crosses to Vincent.*

RHODA. Vincent, dear—sorry, but I need that chair. (*He rises and finds another. Rhoda moves the chair to the end of the circle. She counts the chairs and crosses to Vincent.*) I hate to bother you again, sweetheart, but I need one more chair. (*He rises and starts upstairs.*) Be sure to put a shirt on if you come down while our meeting is going on. And shut the door if you listen to the ballgame. (*He exits. Rhoda calls up the stairs.*) Marigold—are you going to help me straighten up this room or not? (*She arranges different flowering pots critically in various locations. Marigold comes down in a T-shirt that says "Sex Spreads Germs." She starts collecting magazines to be put away.*) Marigold! You're not dressed.
MARIGOLD. I'm not naked.
RHODA. I hope you're not going to serve in that T-shirt.
MARIGOLD. What's wrong with it?
RHODA. "Sex Spreads Germs." Really!
MARIGOLD. Oh, Mother—it's just another one of your hen parties.
RHODA. (*Ecstatically.*) It's a meeting that just may change the whole course of my life. It may mean that I will be Madame President before next Mother's Day.
MARIGOLD. If you wanted to be called Madam, you should have gone into another profession.

RHODA. The trouble with your generation is—you substitute ridicule for respect and use boredom to hide your adolescence as if it were something to be ashamed of.
MARIGOLD. Yes, Mother—and the trouble with your generation is—you forget that you were once our generation. (*She starts to take the book from the mantle and place it back under the coffee table.*)
RHODA. No-no! Leave "Do's and Don't's" just where it is!
MARIGOLD. All right. Don't get in such a tit.
RHODA. The word is *snit*. Oh, go in the kitchen and fix the clam dip. And put an apron over that obscene T-shirt. You can serve canapes when I ring this bell. (*She rings a small bell.*)
MARIGOLD. Yes, Mother. (*Goes into kitchen.*) Repent! The end of the world is at hand!
RHODA. (*Sighs.*) Flowers are better. (*Gets up on footstool to rearrange hanging plant. The doorbell chimes.*) Come in. (*Dillson enters.*) Don't ask me what I'm doing.
DILLSON. I wasn't. I can see. You're flying a kite. Is Marigold in?
RHODA. Yes, but she's busy. I have a meeting here this afternoon so please go home.
DILLSON. It was you I wanted to see, Mrs. Greenleaf.
RHODA. Me? What did you want?
DILLSON. I want to marry Marigold.
RHODA. What did you say?
DILLSON. I said I think me and Marigold ought to get married.
RHODA. I hope you don't mean what I think you mean. Not today.
DILLSON. Oh, she's still a virgin but I think we're wasting valuable time.
RHODA. Dillson—how old are you?
DILLSON. Emotionally, sexually, or chronologically?
RHODA. Fiscally.
DILLSON. Fifteen. (*Adds.*) And-a-half.
RHODA. Dillson—Marigold is almost two years older than you.
DILLSON. Not sexually.
RHODA. How do you know *that?*
DILLSON. School. Sex orientation. The male human animal reaches his highest sexual potential at fifteen. Mice at six weeks. I'm at the peak of my fertility, Mrs. Greenleaf.
RHODA. Dillson—go home. I am not in the mood to discuss *your* fertility. Or mice. Not today.
DILLSON. But it's important, Mrs. Greenleaf. I'd like to marry Marigold by Sunday at the latest.

RHODA. Why Sunday?
DILLSON. School starts Monday.
RHODA. And just what would you live on?
DILLSON. My father.
RHODA. And what makes you think he'd be willing to support you?
DILLSON. He said so. He said he'd pay anything to get me out of the house.
RHODA. Dillson—may I suggest you wait five or six years?
DILLSON. She'll be an old lady.
RHODA. In six years!
DILLSON. Mice are mothers at six weeks.
RHODA. Dillson—we'll discuss mice and senility later—say—in ten years. I'm busy now.
DILLSON. (*Looks around.*) Giving a gang bang?
RHODA. The Garden Club is meeting here and Marigold is helping me serve.
DILLSON. Serve what?
RHODA. What differences does it make? At the moment she's making my clam dip.
DILLSON. Clam dip! I thought that went out with the Republicans. (*Starts for kitchen.*) I'll help her.
RHODA. Dillson—I don't need you!
DILLSON. *She* does. But she's a hold-out. A real frigid-rigid-digit. (*He goes into the kitchen. Rhoda looks heavenward.*)
RHODA. Why, today, O Lord—why today? (*She goes to the phone and dials. Calls into the kitchen while she waits.*) Marigold—keep Socrates locked out of the kitchen—I don't want him racing in here upsetting things. (*Into phone.*) Hello, Cora, dear. Well, this is the big day. I just hope I do everything right. I'm serving potato chips with clam dip. Did that go out with the Republicans? (*Looks up and sees Vincent coming down the stairs in a loud sports shirt.*) Wait a minute, Cora. (*To Vincent as he crosses toward the kitchen.*) If you're going to get a beer, dear, be careful opening the fridge. My shrimp are balanced on top of last night's mulligatawny. (*Vincent nods and goes into the kitchen. Rhoda continues talking to Cora.*) I'm also serving Mexican Gulf shrimp from the Mexican Gulf on gold toothpicks—forty-two dollars worth. Imagine. I don't know what the world's coming to. I can remember when my Uncle Hub was cremated for thirty-five. (*Vincent returns with a can of beer and crosses hurriedly in contrast to his usual lassitude.*) Cora, wait a minute. (*To Vincent.*) Sweetheart—I meant a white shirt—not the flag of Japan.

31

(*He disappears. Rhoda continues.*) Cora—will you pick up Dede and be here first so we can go over everything once more? I don't want anything to go wrong. Thank you, dear. (*Hangs up. Marigold comes in from the kitchen. Dillson stands behind her. She has on an apron that covers her T-shirt.*)
MARIGOLD. Mother—do you want to come in the kitchen?
RHODA. No—I do *not*. Why?
MARIGOLD. Dad knocked over your shrimp. They fell into the mulligatawny.
RHODA. I'll kill that man. I will.
MARIGOLD. What do I do? Serve shrimp soup?
RHODA. Did they *all* fall in the soup?
DILLSON. No. You were lucky. Some fell on the floor.
MARIGOLD. Do you want to come in and look?
RHODA. No—I don't want to come in and look. Fish them out of the soup and pick the rest off the floor and wash them under the faucet. Are you helpless!
MARIGOLD. Just thought I'd ask. No need to get in a tit. (*She and Dillson exit.*)
RHODA. Snit! Snit! Tit is a mammary gland! You'll never get into Vassar. (*Goes to phone and dials.*) I should have become a nun like my cousin and devoted my life to pollinating Sleeping Virgins. (*Then, into phone.*) Hello, Evie? Rhoda. Is your Pussy Toes in bloom? Could I borrow it for my party? This room seems so barren. (*It isn't.*) Oh thank you. I'll give you a beautiful Busy Lizzie for Christmas. 'Bye. (*Hangs up. Dillson enters alone.*)
DILLSON. Mrs. Greenleaf—there's something you ought to know.
RHODA. There are a lot of things I ought to know. Why you don't go home is one.
DILLSON. Socrates made a hole in the screen door.
RHODA. Then lock him in the basement.
DILLSON. There's something else you ought to know.
RHODA. Yes—why I ever let Marigold bring that dog home in the first place.
DILLSON. He ate the shrimp on the floor while we were in here.
RHODA. I'll kill that dog. I will. Forty-two dollars. Uncle Hub will turn over in his ashes.
DILLSON. That's not all, Mrs. Greenleaf.
RHODA. He ate the clam dip?
DILLSON. No. He threw up. It's a mess.
RHODA. Well, tell Marigold to clean it up. I haven't time to bother.

DILLSON. She says she can't. *She'll* throw up.
RHODA. All right. Then *you* clean it up!
DILLSON. I can't. *I'll* throw up.
RHODA. (*Starts for kitchen.*) Why don't you elope with my daughter right away—I'll give you a dog for a wedding present. (*They go out. The doorbell chimes. There is a wait and Cora enters with Dede.*)
CORA. Rhoda?
DEDE. She must be in the kitchen.
CORA. (*Calls.*) It's me, Rhoda—the Bride of Frankenstein.
DEDE. Aren't you the one!
RHODA. (*Offstage.*) Be right in.
CORA. Well, this is D-Day. "D" for "Do's and Don't's."
DEDE. Oh, I better make sure it's here. (*Goes to mantel.*) It's here.
CORA. I've got five pledges to vote for the motion. How many did you get?
DEDE. Four.
CORA. You didn't tell anybody what this motion would be, did you?
DEDE. Oh, no. Of course. Just Thelma.
CORA. You told Thelma Rittenhouse?
DEDE. She wouldn't give me her pledge unless she knew what it was for.
CORA. She's a friend of Lillybelle's!
DEDE. I made her swear on her Bible she wouldn't tell Lillybelle.
CORA. She's an atheist. She hasn't *got* a Bible!
DEDE. She swore on her Exotica.
CORA. Her what?
DEDE. You know—her Horticultural Encyclopedia.
CORA. Well, don't tell Rhoda. It'll just upset her. I wouldn't trust Thelma Rittenhouse with my garbage.
DEDE. Thelma wouldn't say anything. She's a very trustworthy atheist. (*Goes to plant.*) Hello, Fluffy Ruffle. (*To another plant.*) How are you, Violet? (*To another.*) Good morning, Lily. (*To another.*) Hi, Hibiscus. (*Rhoda enters.*)
RHODA. Dede, do you really believe plants can understand you. How does an African Violet know English?
DEDE. (*Loftily.*) Flowers are the universal language of love.
CORA. I wish I'd said that. (*Marigold comes to kitchen door.*)
MARIGOLD. Mother—excuse me. I've opened the sardines. What do you want them on?
RHODA. On a platter, dear. What did you *think* I wanted them on, a piece of paper?
MARIGOLD. I don't know. I can't read your mind.

RHODA. You're lucky. Go down in the basement and get my Spode platter—the one that your Grandmother Pugh left us. Do you know where to look?
MARIGOLD. All I know is they're both buried somewhere. (*Goes out. Rhoda turns back to her guests.*)
RHODA. I've got something wonderful to show you. (*Goes to a small stand and returns with small pot.*) Look. It's up!
CORA. *What's* up?
RHODA. My Sleeping Virgin. I planted both bulbs but only one came up. There's not another one in the whole United States.
CORA. One virgin. That's a sad commentary on this country.
DEDE. Oh, Cora—you're awful. (*There is a crash heard from the kitchen, followed by the yelp of a dog.*)
CORA. What was that?
RHODA. I don't want to know. I don't ever want to know.
DEDE. Sounds like someone stepped on Socrates.
RHODA. I hope so. Ignore it. (*The door chime is heard. Rhoda starts for the door.*)
DEDE. It's a perfect day for the meeting. The oleanders are out.
RHODA. With my luck so far—it'll rain. (*Opens door. Evie, Dora, Clara and Birdie enter. Evie carries a potted plant.*) Oh! Welcome, everyone. (*There is a general exchange of hellos.*)
EVIE. Here's your Pussy Toes. We decided to all come together. I've nicknamed us The Fearless Foursome.
DORA. That's what she nicknamed us—"The Fearless Foursome."
RHODA. Well, I'm glad. And if I get to be President—I'll know who to thank.
CORA. Your Sleeping Virgin. The only one left.
BIRDIE. (*Shouts.*) What'd she say?
CORA. (*Shouts.*) She has the one and only known Sleeping Virgin in the entire United States.
BIRDIE. Then she hasn't been to Boston.
CLARA. I wish it had another generic term. It's a noun that I find needlessly graphic.
BIRDIE. It may be a noun to you, dear, but to the rest of us—it's a verb—past tense. (*Dillson comes to the kitchen door.*)
DILLSON. Mrs. Greenleaf, could I see you a moment.
RHODA. You see me now. What do you want?
DILLSON. We had a little accident.
RHODA. Somehow, I'm not at all surprised. What is it?
DILLSON. Not much. Only Marigold went down in the basement

to get that Spode platter you wanted and tripped over Socrates. She hurt her leg.
RHODA. Well—at least it wasn't broken. That's all I need.
DILLSON. Oh, but it was. It broke into a million pieces.
RHODA. I trust you mean the Spode.
DILLSON. (*Nods.*) She wants to know what to put the sardines on now.
RHODA. Tell her to put them on anything and not to bother me.
DILLSON. Like you say. (*Waves to his mother.*) Hi, Mom. (*He goes out.*)
CORA. I had a little accident fifteen years ago. That's him.
RHODA. Everything has gone wrong for me today.
CLARA. Today went wrong for Joan of Arc, too.
EVIE. I don't want to be pessimistic, Rhoda, but I looked up your horoscope today. It said "Beware of scuba diving and false friends."
DORA. It did, too.
RHODA. Well, I can't turn the clock back. Now—how many pledges have we got?
EVIE. Dora and I have nine between us.
DORA. Five and four—that's nine.
DEDE. Three.
CORA. Seven.
CLARA. One.
BIRDIE. Eight.
RHODA. Birdie! How did you get eight promises?
BIRDIE. I told them I'd leave them something in my will. And I will. My goodwill.
CORA. You're safe. You'll outlive us all. You're that stubborn.
BIRDIE. Yes, dear. If you get to hell first, wait for me. (*The door chime rings.*)
RHODA. (*Starts for door.*) You didn't—any of you—tell what this motion was for, did you?
TOGETHER. No—no—no—no!
RHODA. (*Opens door.*) Agnes! How are you, dear? (*Agnes, a rather fat matron, enters beaming radiantly.*)
AGNES. Hello, Rhoda. Hi, everyone. Guess what! I got my dykia! (Dick-ia)
BIRDIE. (*Shouts.*) What'd she get?
CORA. (*Shouts.*) Her dykia.
AGNES. I can't wait to get it in the ground.
BIRDIE. Well, that's where they all end up.

CLARA. Agnes, dear—that's pronounced *Dié*-kia.
AGNES. (*Airily.*) Dick—dyke—they sound alike. What difference does it make?
CLARA. Well, we like to be correct in a Garden Club, dear. After all, if you had a friend named Gussie—you wouldn't call her Goosie, would you?
AGNES. I might. (*The door bell chimes. Rhoda goes to it.*)
DEDE. (*To Agnes.*) Did you see Rhoda's Polypody? (*Points.*) Doesn't it give you duck-bumps?
RHODA. (*Opens door. Six club members, Ada, Ginger, Celeste, Emily, Madge and Sophie, enter in a group.*) Hi, girls. Come on in. (*They file in amidst a general confusion of "Hi"'s and hugs.*)
GINGER. Hello, Birdie. (*Sits beside her.*) Where have you been? I've missed you at the supermarket.
CORA. She went to a funeral in Boston.
GINGER. I go to as many funerals as I can. I check them out in the obituaries. You can steal wonderful cuttings from the flowers people send.
DEDE. Doesn't anyone stop you?
GINGER. Everyone thinks you're collecting a memento. No one knows who you are at a funeral. Or cares. Including the deceased.
CLARA. You don't even know who's being buried?
GINGER. Why? It's too late to do anything about it then. Last week I went to a Mafia funeral in Hoboken and I got a Golden Birdnest Sansevieria.
BIRDIE. (*Shouts.*) What'd she say?
CORA. She's been to a funeral, too.
BIRDIE. (*Shouts.*) Anybody we know?
DEDE. (*Shouts.*) Total stranger.
BIRDIE. (*Shouts.*) She run over somebody?
CORA. (*Shouts.*) She went for a Golden Birdnest.
BIRDIE. (*Stares at her.*) Nothing makes any sense anymore. Sounded just like she said she went for a Golden Birdnest. I think I'll take a nap. (*She folds her arms and closes her eyes. The door chime is heard. Rhoda crosses to door.*)
SOPHIE. (*To Madge as Rhoda crosses.*) Madge, do you have brown scale on your ferns, dear?
MADGE. No, but I'm getting liver spots on my hands. (*Shows her hands.*)
SOPHIE. Well, there's no insecticide for *that*.
MADGE. I know. But there's always suicide. (*Rhoda opens door.*

Louise, Zelda, Harriet, Bertha, Susan and Judi enter amid hugs and "Hi"'s.)
RHODA. Welcome, girls—come on in!
JUDI. Are we late?
RHODA. No—the tribe is just gathering. The fertility dance hasn't started yet.
BERTHA. Hi, Ada—how are your tubers?
ADA. Don't ask. I'm low man on the flower totem.
ZELDA. Does anybody here have an Exotica?
EMILY. *I* do, why?
ZELDA. Will you look up ananas bracteatus striatus and tell me the proper pronunciation?
EMILY. How do you spell it?
ZELDA. Oh, god! Why did you ask! Never mind. (*The door chimes again. Rhoda starts for the door.*)
CELESTE. (*To Susan.*) I asked her cook for the recipe and she said—Well, ma'am, you jes' take a cup of flour, half a stick of butter, a tablespoon of sugar and a mouthful of water.
SUSAN. I'll skip it. (*Rhoda opens door. Francine, Vi, Stella, Trudi, Vera, Margaret, Lorraine, Besse, and Rita enter chattering.*)
RHODA. Come in, girls. Join the Girl Scouts. (*There are the usual mixed greetings and kisses blown.*)
STELLA. Where's Lillybelle, Rhoda? Isn't she here yet?
LORRAINE. We can't start without her.
STELLA. She always reminds me of a proud white oleander.
CORA. Yes—proud and poisonous.
RHODA. Well, I can start with the canapés while we wait. (*Rings her bell.*)
BESSIE. What if Lillybelle doesn't show up? We can't have a meeting without the President, can we?
VERA. Oh, she'll be here. She went to her hair dresser yesterday. She won't waste that on her gardenias. (*Marigold enters with a tray of shrimp. Dillson follows with the chips and dip. Marigold limps to the table and puts the platter down. Dillson taps one lady on the shoulder and points to the canapés.*)
DILLSON: Clam dip—Republican's Delight.
RHODA. *I'll* do that. (*She takes the platter away from him. Marigold limps out.*)
VI. (*To Dillson.*) Why is Marigold limping, Dillson? Did she hurt herself?
DILLSON. Naw—she was born with a short leg. (*He goes out.*)

RHODA. Here—have some shrimp. They're Mexican Gulf Shrimp from the Gulf of Mexico.
RITA. Oh, "D" for delicious. *Whatever* did you do to the shrimp?
RHODA. I dip them in Mulligatatwany. It's a family discovery. (*While Rhoda passes the canapes, our attention goes to Fran and Dorothy across the room by the fireplace. Fran picks up the book on the mantel.*)
FRAN. Oh, look—here's "Do's and Don't's for Dahlias." I've been dying to read this. (*She thumbs through the pages.*)
DOROTHY. (*Smugly.*) I have it. It's my bible.
FRAN. Do you have "The Battle for Begonias"?
DOROTHY. My dear, I have *everything*. (*Counts on her fingers.*) "Fighting Fungus"—"Marching With Marigolds"—"Do It With Dogwood"—"How to Live With Lilies" and "I Found God in Gladiolas." The Library of Congress is *green* with envy.
FRAN. (*Taps book.*) Well, I want to look up what to do for dew-worm. I've a very, very sick dahlia.
DOROTHY. Look on the bright side, dear. We all have to go sometime. (*Fran takes the book and goes* u. *to an obscure corner and settles down to read "Do's and Don't's."*)
ZELDA. Rhoda, old Mrs. Smithers is sound asleep. Do you think we should wake her for a shrimp?
RHODA. Only if there's a fire—she wouldn't want to miss it.
ZELDA. (*Gazing down at Birdie.*) Poor old thing. Her face is like a road map—all those lines telling you where to go. Do you suppose she was really a lovely queen at sweet sixteen?
BIRDIE. (*Opens her eyes.*) Of course I was—you damned fool. If you're not a queen at sixteen—had your fun by twenty-one—could copulate at thirty-eight and learn new tricks by forty-six or something new at fifty two—satisfied by seventy and still alive at eighty-five—then you've earned your road map. Who wants a skin like a baby's butt with just about as much character? And as for those lines on my map telling you how to get someplace, mine are telling you to go to hell. Don't wake me up again. (*She folds her arms and closes her eyes again. Rhoda pats her affectionately, then turns to go to the door as the chimes are sounded.*)
CORA. That must be Lillybelle. She likes to create suspense—like ground-hog day.
ZELDA. Good. Maybe we can get started. I've got to get home and put my bottom round on.
RHODA. (*Opens door.*) Oh, hello, Angelica. Come in, dear—we're nearly all here. (*Angelica enters. She considers herself very sexy. And she was—a few years back.*)

ANGELICA. *(Waves.)* Hi, girls. I know I'm late but you'll never guess why.
CORA. Is there a prize?
ANGELICA. It's just *too* delicious. You know that Immaculate Conception Church on the corner of Spook Rock and Pussywillow?
ZELDA. Of course. You'll find me there every Saturday night.
CORA. For confession?
ZELDA. No, bingo.
ANGELICA. Well, Sundays they put a new officer there to direct traffic. Well, I put out my hand to make a turn and do you know what?
CORA. What?
ANGELICA. He kissed it. That handsome young traffic cop kissed it. My hand.
RHODA. No!
ANGELICA. Yes!
RHODA. What did you do?
ANGELICA. I did what any self-respecting woman my age would do. I drove around the corner and put my hand out again.
CORA. Did he kiss it again?
ANGELICA. No—he gave me a ticket.
DEDE. Oh, that was *mean.*
ANGELICA. Not at all. It was a ticket to the Policeman's Ball.
RHODA. You're not going, are you!
ANGELICA. Try and stop me.
CLARA. Try *to* stop me is correct grammar. *(Adds.)* If not your behavior.
CORA. You shouldn't have told us. We'll all drive home that way.
ANGELICA. Isn't Lillybelle here?
RHODA. Not yet.
ANGELICA. Well, we can't have a meeting unless the President presides, can we?
RHODA. That just occurred to me.
CORA. Call her house and see if anything is wrong. *(Rhoda starts for the phone. The doorbell chimes.)*
CORA. *That* must be her. I felt an earth tremor. *(Rhoda starts for the door.)*
ANGELICA. Maybe she's sent her gardener to tell us she's sick. If it is, Rhoda, ask him in—he's terribly good looking.
RHODA. *(Opens door.)* Lillybelle! We thought you'd forgotten.
LILLYBELLE. Oh, "nev-air." Bon jour—girls—sorry I'm late but better late than never, as Queen Zenobia said.

DEDE. (*Skeptically.*) Zenobia? When did she say that?
LILLYBELLE. When she remarried at ninety. I thought you'd never ask. (*Laughs gaily.*)
ANGELICA. Oh, Lillybelle—you have such a wonderful sense of humor.
LILLYBELLE. Well, when you're not pretty you have to be witty, mon chéri. (*To Rhoda.*) What's new and exciting with you, Rhoda dear?
RHODA. Oh, cut worms and mealy bugs. What have *you* been up to, dear?
LILLYBELLE. Oh, being President of the Garden Club takes up so much of my time. You'll never know, Sweetie.
RHODA. Well, things might change for the better, dear. Who knows?
LILLYBELLE. Yes—as you say—"Qui sais." (*To gathering.*) Well, why don't we start our meeting. Thelma Rittenhouse won't be here. She phoned me. Girls—girls! Will you all be seated—s'il vous plaît. Merci. (*As the members begin to seat themselves, two of the "girls" are overheard finishing a conversation as they stand* D.L.)
AGNES. I adore Jane but she's a terrible housekeeper. Do you know all her pictures on the walls have *layers* of dust on top of the frames?
GINGER. How did you happen to notice a thing like that?
AGNES. I stood on a chair. (*They turn to take seats and our attention shifts to the Opposite Side of the stage where two other "girls" are finishing their gossip.*)
MADGE. Why do you suppose Lorraine dyes her hair *white*? She's not old enough for that yet.
TRUDI. My dear! Didn't you know? She found her husband Charles in bed with his secretary. So she quickly had it dyed so she could tell him that her hair had turned *white* overnight.
MADGE. Did it help her marriage?
TRUDI. No—but it helped her divorce. The Judge awarded her triple alimony.
MADGE. That must have been a blow to Charles.
TRUDI. It was. His hair turned white overnight. (*They have all found seats and Lillybelle and Clara have taken their place behind the card table.*)
CORA. Birdie has fallen asleep again.
RHODA. Don't wake her. We'll get thru quicker.
LILLYBELLE. (*Hammers with gavel.*) "Garde à vous—s'il vou plaît. Merci beaucoup." The twenty-eighth meeting of the Upper

South Ho-Ho-Kus Little Lake Garden Club will now come to order. As usual we will begin with our own Club Song. (*To Zelda.*) Zelda—will you give us the pitch? (*Zelda blows the proper note on a whistle. They stand and all sing.*)
ALL.
"OH, WE ARE GIRLS OF THE GARDEN CLUB
FRIENDS OF FLOWERS
SPENDING HOURS
PLANTING FLORA, FERN AND SHRUB
ARMED WITH FLIT GUN
IN THE HOT SUN
WE ARE SOLDIERS OF SEED AND SOIL.

"OH, WE ARE WARRIORS FOR THIS NATION
WE PRUNE AND ROOT
WE DON'T POLLUTE
WE DEPLORE DEFOLIATION
BUGS THAT EAT US
CAN'T DEFEAT US
FIGHTING THE FIGHT FOR CONSERVATION.

"OH, WE ARE SISTERS, DEDICATED
CLARA. (*Alone.*)
IN MUD AND MUCK
WE PICK AND PLUCK
ALL.
TO SEE THAT PLANTS ARE PROPAGATED
ZELDA. (*Alone.*)
WE WORK AND TOIL
IN BARREN SOIL
ALL.
TO US OUR DIRT IS CONSECRATED
OH, GIRLS OF THE GARDEN CLUB ARE WE
ARE WE—ARE WE
WE ARE!"
(*There is a round of applause. Birdie wakes up.*)
BIRDIE. (*Alarmed.*) What's happened?
EVIE. We just sang our song.
DORA. Together.
BIRDIE. Glad I missed it.
LILLYBELLE. Now—we'll cover the business at hand. Celeste, you're on the Cook Book committee—will you report, "s'il vou plait"? (*She sits as Celeste rises.*)

CELESTE. Well, as you girls all know, we plan to publish our Garden Club Cook Book with recipes from members. So far I've received eighteen recipes for tunafish loaf and fourteen for apple pandowdy. Also I have received ten recipes for a dessert that bothers me. It's made with leftover rice and prunes. It's called Poor Man's Pudding and it seems to me that name might be offensive to those poor people on food stamps.
BIRDIE. (*Aside to Cora.*) Doesn't that damn fool know people on food stamps don't read cook books? They eat 'em.
LILLYBELLE. (*Rises.*) Which reminds me—excuse me, Celeste—but I've been worried a long time about the name Wandering Jew being offensive to our dear friends of the Jewish faith. I would like this Club to lead the way and call it Migratory Yehudi.
BIRDIE. I knew a Yehudi—played the violin.
LILLYBELLE. And since that's biblical, no one could possibly take offense.
CLARA. Does anybody second the motion?
ZELDA. I second it. Oh, Lillybelle, aren't you wonderful! It's a milestone for Upper South Ho-Ho-Kus Little Lake.
LILLYBELLE. (*Smirks.*) "Merci beaucoup." (*Sits.*)
CLARA. Motion carried.
LILLYBELLE. (*To Celeste.*) Go ahead, dear.
CELESTE. Well, that was all. Shall we try again, girls? I'd like to see some exciting recipes for Jello. Thank you. (*She sits. Lillybelle rises.*)
LILLYBELLE. "Merci," Celeste. Now. (*Looks at her program.*) Zelda—as Flower Chairwoman, would you tell us what you have learned about drying and dying?
ZELDA. (*Rises.*) Well, as we all know, dried flowers are *in* again. A few years ago, they were *out*. But now they're *in* again.
BIRDIE. Like the Democrats.
ZELDA. They should be hung, heads down in the sun.
BIRDIE. Like the Democrats.
ZELDA. As to colors—green is ideal for dried carnations on St. Patrick's Day.
BIRDIE. Ever try to dry out an Irishman?
ZELDA. Butcher's Broom or Bristol Fairy is lovely when dyed red. You can put it on anything.
BIRDIE. Except ice cream.
ZELDA. So be adventurous, girls. Pick your dye, dry and dip. (*She sits down. Lillybelle rises.*)
LILLYBELLE. Now we have the awards from our last meeting.

The subject was "My favorite bird and how it sounds." First prize has been voted to Margaret Looslip—a stainless steel asparagus knife. Margaret, would you like to demonstrate the bird call that won you first prize? *(Margaret rises. Lillybelle sits.)*
MARGARET. As you may recall, my favorite bird was the Yellow-bellied Wallet. This lovely bird has three distinct calls. The morning call, the evening call and the mating call. First—the morning call. *(She sips a glass of water and clears her throat.)* I'm not in very good voice today. I ate a bad oyster. The morning call. *(She imitates a bird. Any bird. Vincent comes down the stairs a couple of steps to stare.)* The evening call. *(She repeats practically the same sound. Vincent goes back upstairs.)* The mating call to the female Wallet. *(She gives the same whistle.)*
BIRDIE. If I was Wallet, I wouldn't answer. *(There is applause as Margaret sits down.)*
LILLYBELLE. Honorable Mention was awarded to Francine Buckelmaster. Francine, are you in good voice, "mon chéri"?
FRANCINE. *(Rises.)* I'll try. My bird was the Red, White and Blue Bunting. It has two calls. The female answers to both. The sunrise call sounds something like this. *(She whistles. Vincent in hat and coat comes down the stairs and sneaks out during the applause.)* The night call sounds like this. *(She whistles. She simpers modestly and sits.)*
BIRDIE. Ask me—she laid an egg.
LILLYBELLE. Now, unless anybody has any motions to make, the club business can be concluded, I hereby declare this meeting "Fini."
RHODA. *(The opportune moment for Rhoda has arrived. She leaps to her feet.)* Would anybody like some cranberry juice? *(Dede dashes to get the assigned book. When she finds it missing, she turns to Rhoda and shrugs helplessly.)*
LILLYBELLE. I think I would, Rhoda—with just a "soupçon" of vodka, "s'il vou plaît."
DEDE. *(Races back to Rhoda.)* "Do" and Don'ts" has disappeared!
RHODA. Never mind—grab any book. Hurry. *(She races back, snatching up a book from the coffee table on the way. Rhoda repeats.)* Would anybody else like any cranberry juice?
DEDE. *(Composed at the mantel, she gives her squeal of delight.)* Girls—girls! I would like to recommend this wonderful book called—*(She glances down at the title and pales.)* the—the Bible.
CORA. *(Stands on footstool as rehearsed.)* Girls—girls. I would also like to make a recommendation—
LILLYBELLE. *(Interrupts.)* So would I, Cora dear. But as Presi-

dent, I would like to make *mine* first because it affects the Presidency. I would like to make a motion that we change the voting rules this year. I think only the best gardener should be President so I make the motion that whoever wins first prize at this year's Flower Show will automatically become our new President. (*Rhoda sinks into a chair beside Birdie, thunderstruck.*)
ZELDA. I think that's a wonderful idea, Lillybelle.
AGNES. So unselfish. I second the motion.
CLARA. Anyone opposed? Motion carried.
CORA. (*To Rhoda.*) Rhoda! She's stolen your thunder and taking credit.
RHODA. It doesn't matter. I still have the only way anyone can win.
ZELDA. Lillybelle—it's a wonderful idea but we don't want to lose you as President. What if you don't get first prize?
LILLYBELLE. Oh, I think I will. You see I have a brother-in-law in Burma at the Consul's office. He's sent me some very rare bulbs called Sleeping Virgin. (*She holds up her bulbs.*)
BIRDIE. Rhoda! She's got your testicles!
LILLYBELLE. They're only grown in the King's Garden and there's no other Sleeping Virgin bulbs in this country.
CORA. Can I get you a drink, Rhoda?
RHODA. Yes—poison on the rocks.
LILLYBELLE. (*To all.*) So I'm not worried, "tout le monde." I shall again ride triumphantly to the Presidency on my two trusty bulbs. "C'est le guerre!" (*There is general applause. Rhoda sits stunned. Birdie pats her hand sympathetically. Dora comes over to her.*)
DORA. Rhoda—could *I* have some cranberry juice?

CURTAIN

ACT THREE

Scene 1

PLACE: *The Same.*
TIME: *Day of the Flower Show.*
AT RISE: *When the curtain rises, we see a two-foot plant revealed* C. *on a small stand. It is featured in a circle of light. The Sleeping Virgin has awakened. It is resplendent in spectacular blossom (plastic or paper). Slowly, the lighting for the rest of the room is brought up to normal level.*
After a moment Rhoda enters from the patio with spray-gun and watering can.
She sprays the plant with carefully measured bursts of spray and waters it with the caution of a trained nurse.

RHODA. Wake up, little Sleeping Virgin. This is your wedding day. (*She puts the can aside and calls upstairs.*) Marigold! (*She stands, beaming down at her plant. Marigold enters from the kitchen instead.*)
MARIGOLD. Yes, Mother Earth.
RHODA. Isn't it beautiful!
MARIGOLD. You see one Virgin—you've seen 'em all.
RHODA. Oh, no, Dillson reports that Lillybelle's Virgin is only half this size.
MARIGOLD. (*Shrugs.*) Some like 'em big—some like 'em little.
RHODA. What a pity you have no affinity for flowers. I should never have named you Marigold. It was wasted.
MARIGOLD. So was yours. You should have married someone named Dendron. Then you'd have been called Rhodadendron.
RHODA. Very funny. Well, I'm going up to get dressed for the Flower Show. (*Starts up the stairs.*) I wanted to warn you not to open the patio door. There's a breeze and I don't want my prize-winning plant to catch a cold. (*She exits. Marigold stares down at the plant.*)
MARIGOLD. Oh, you're not so special. I'm a virgin, too, but I don't expect any prize. I'd only have to give it back sooner or later. (*She starts for the kitchen as the door opens and Dillson enters with a shoe box.*)

DILLSON. Psst! (*Marigold turns. Dillson puts a finger to his lips.*) Ssh! (*He tiptoes toward her.*) Where's your Mother?

MARIGOLD. Upstairs putting on her eyelashes and her party smile.

DILLSON. I've got a great plan to give her morale a goose before the Flower Show.

MARIGOLD. I don't know what you're talking about but I already don't like it.

DILLSON. What gives a person faith? A miracle. So I'm going to set up a miracle for her. (*He opens his shoe box.*)

MARIGOLD. Who do you think you are? God?

DILLSON. Who wants to be God? There's no chance for promotion. My faith is science. This. (*Holds up a small mike and some wire.*) Since she's started talking to her plant, I'm going to plant this mike in her plant so it can talk back to her. (*He starts arranging the microphone in the plant stand.*)

MARIGOLD. Do you expect her to believe it?

DILLSON. (*Pompously.*) Faith is believing the impossible.

MARIGOLD. And just where did you learn that?

DILLSON. Theology Two—it's right after Sex Orientation. It's worth taking if you want to sleep.

MARIGOLD. Do you know how to hook it up?

DILLSON. Of course. I'm a genius. I fixed up one from my bed down to our kitchen so I could tell Mom when I'm ready for breakfast. I took T.V. Repair. It's just before Sex Orientation. (*Hands her some wire.*) Here—help me hide it under the rug.

MARIGOLD. (*Helps him plant the wire leading into the kitchen.*) I don't think this is a good idea. She's nervous enough.

DILLSON. Why not? Think of how set up she'll be with a talking plant to take to the Flower Show. (*At kitchen.*) Now. Let's test it. Go over and stand by the plant and say something. (*He darts into the kitchen. Marigold crosses to the plant.*)

MARIGOLD. What'll I say?

DILLSON. (*Offstage.*) Anything. What God hath wrought. Damn the torpedoes. Anything. Hurry up.

MARIGOLD. I've never talked to a plant before. (*Clears her throat.*) Hello, Virgin.

DILLSON. (*His high-pitched voice is heard thru the plant.*) Hello, Rhoda.

MARIGOLD. You don't sound like a flower to me.

DILLSON. (*Thru plant in his own voice.*) Say something else.

MARIGOLD.
"Pussy cat, pussy cat, where have you been
I've been to London to visit the Queen
Pussy cat, pussy cat, what did—?"
DILLSON. (*Sticks head out door to interrupt.*) That's fine. Come on, get out of sight, pussy cat. And for Pete's sake—don't break up laughing. (*They both disappear into the kitchen. After a moment, Rhoda comes down the stairs with her hat on and carrying her purse. She goes to the phone and dials. She checks her appearance in her purse mirror as she waits.*)
RHODA. Hello, Cora, are you ready to pick me up? I'm ready. Of course, I'm nervous as a cat. I'm going to take a little nip of sherry to give me courage. By-by. See you in a minute. (*She hangs up and gets a sherry bottle. She pours herself a drink. She sips it and crosses down to the plant. To plant.*) Well, this is zero hour for us, my little beauty. I certainly hope we win. (*She turns to put the glass down.*)
PLANT. (*High voice.*) Me, too. (*Rhoda freezes. She stands for a long moment with her back to the audience. She turns her head slowly to look over her shoulder at the plant. Then she turns her whole body—stares at the plant and scans the room. She then leans over the plant—her face close to the leaves.*)
RHODA. Did—did you—speak to me?
PLANT. That's right. (*Rhoda backs up and stumbles backward into a chair. She swallows her Adam's apple and feels her heart. She quickly downs the rest of her drink. She rises and goes to the plant again.*)
RHODA. You—you can talk!
PLANT. Why not? You talk to me.
RHODA. Oh, good Lord—I don't believe it. (*Puts her hands to her head.*)
PLANT. That's what St. Thomas said to the Lord, too. A doubting Thomas.
RHODA. (*Looks up.*) You—you know the Bible!
PLANT. Of course. God created us before he did you. You were later—the sixth day.
RHODA. It's a miracle! A miracle! (*Calls.*) Marigold! Marigold—come here—quick!
MARIGOLD. (*Enters.*) What's the matter, Mother?
RHODA. (*Grabs her.*) Do you believe in miracles?
MARIGOLD. Well, the Democrats are in.
RHODA. Do you believe the dead can come to life?
MARIGOLD. I know a few.
RHODA. Would you believe a talking plant?
MARIGOLD. Why not? Parrots talk.

RHODA. Well, I want you to witness a miracle. You've called me a Flower Freak—a Zinnia Zealot—and a Caladium Kook. Now, you'll see how crazy I am. Listen. (*She turns to the plant and speaks jauntily.*) Hello, dear. (*She waits.*) Hello, plant. (*No answer.*)
MARIGOLD. I agree. You're crazy. (*Starts back.*)
RHODA. Wait a minute! (*To plant.*) Hello. (*Waits.*) Hello, dear. (*Waits.*) Hello, Virgin.
MARIGOLD. There's no one there, Mother. Hang up. (*She goes back into kitchen.*)
RHODA. (*To plant.*) Why didn't you answer!
PLANT. I'm shy.
RHODA. You don't have to be shy with me. I'm your mother.
PLANT. Could I have a drink?
RHODA. A drink? I just watered you.
PLANT. I mean what *you're* drinking.
RHODA. You want some sherry?
PLANT. I'm nervous too. Virgins are always nervous.
RHODA. You drink wine?
PLANT. I *hate* manure.
RHODA. Well, just a little, then. (*She pours a few drops.*)
PLANT. More.
RHODA. Should you?
PLANT. More.
RHODA. (*Empties the whole glass.*) I hope to heaven you don't wither.
PLANT. More.
RHODA. No. We both have to be seen in public. (*The door opens as Cora lets herself in. Clara follows.*)
CORA. I brought my car. I thought your plant might be happier in the station wagon.
RHODA. Cora, Clara—come here. I want you to witness a miracle.
CORA. Well, it's certainly grown but I wouldn't call it a miracle.
RHODA. Cora—it can talk.
CORA. Of course. Say it with flowers.
CLARA. But not to be taken literally.
RHODA. No. It speaks. (*Adds.*) English. (*Turns to plant.*) Listen. (*Pats the pot.*) Say hello to Cora. (*Waits.*) Please say hello. (*Waits.*) Speak! Speak!
CLARA. (*Lifts decanter accusingly.*) Rhoda. I'm surprised at you. And just before the Flower Show.

RHODA. I tell you the plant spoke to me! I heard it.
CLARA. Some people see snakes.
CORA. What did it say?
RHODA. It quoted the Bible.
CORA. (*Puts bottle back on the table.*) I don't think you'd better have any more, dear. The Judge is a Christian Scientist. He doesn't *believe* in drinking. (*Picks up plant and goes to door.*)
CLARA. Come, Rhoda. The fresh air will do you good.
RHODA. Very well. You'll see. When the judges come around and my plant says hello, he'll become a Catholic. *They* believe in miracles. (*They go out. Marigold and Dillson come in giggling.*)
MARIGOLD. I can't believe she believed it.
DILLSON. I told you—faith is believing the impossible. That's how we got to the moon.
MARIGOLD. And you'd better go there if she finds out.
DILLSON. (*Kneels to remove mike from stand.*) You know—in a million years from now, human beings aren't going to talk at all. They'll just exchange mental radio messages. And you know who'll talk? Dogs.
MARIGOLD. Then who'll bark? Fish? (*The door opens and Rhoda returns dejectedly. Dillson gets quickly to his feet.*) Mother—what's the matter? You'll be late for the Flower Show.
RHODA. I'm not going.
MARIGOLD. Don't you want to win first prize?
RHODA. I wouldn't win it.
MARIGOLD. Why not?
RHODA. As we were putting my plant into the station wagon, it suddenly wilted. Collapsed. Melted like a dish of tutti-fruitti ice cream.
DILLSON. You mean—it died—that sudden?
RHODA. Wait. (*Turns to door. Cora and Clara return carrying the plant. The leaves have drooped dejectedly and the blossoms are closed. NOTE: Use duplicate plant.*) There. Look! My Sleeping Virgin went back to sleep.
CORA. I couldn't have been more surprised. (*Puts plant back on stand.*)
CLARA. Actually, *I'm* not surprised. It was today that Napoleon lost at Waterloo.
RHODA. And this is *my* Waterloo. I've lost to Lillybelle instead of England.
CORA. I can't imagine what happened to it!

RHODA. (*To plant.*) What's the matter with you? Speak up. Tell us. Don't be shy. It's your mother speaking.
CORA. Sometimes—I've heard—if you dissolve an aspirin in warm water and pour it on the roots, it'll revive the plant.
CLARA. Marigold—get an aspirin.
RHODA. Get me one, too. (*Marigold dashes out.*)
CORA. Rhoda, if the aspirin doesn't help—do you have another plant you can send? You ought to enter something.
RHODA. Yes. A convent.
CLARA. Any other plant will do.
RHODA. What? A polypody? A Migratory Yehudi? Some parsley?
MARIGOLD. (*Returns with two glasses. Hands one to Cora.*) I've already dissolved the aspirin. (*Hands mother second glass.*) One or two, Mother?
RHODA. The whole bottle. (*Holds up glass.*) What is this? Blood?
MARIGOLD. Cranberry juice. I thought it would help. (*Rhoda downs her pill.*)
CORA. Well, here goes. (*Cora pours her liquid on the plant. They all watch it intently.*)
RHODA. Do you think we should call for an oxygen tent? (*Pours herself more sherry.*)
CLARA. I don't think you should drink that, Rhoda. I read where somebody drank sherry with aspirin and died.
RHODA. It's alright. I want to die. (*Downs drink.*)
CORA. (*Looking at plant.*) It doesn't seem to be helping. But I'm sure it will be all right by tomorrow.
RHODA. That'll be too late.
CORA. Let's take it anyhow. It might revive on the way. Come on, girls.
RHODA. Not me. I don't want to be humiliated in front of Lillybelle, I want to be humiliated at home where I'm comfortable.
CORA. Then *we'll* take it. Cheer up, Rhoda. Things are not always as bad as they seem.
CLARA. She's right. Sometimes they're worse.
CORA. Oh, come on, Clara! (*Goes to door with plant.*) We'll still enter it in your name, dear.
CLARA. (*At door.*) Rhoda, there was something else that I wasn't going to tell you today but since you feel so awful anyhow, you might as well know it now. Today is the day the Titanic sank. (*She goes out.*)

RHODA. The Titanic and me.
MARIGOLD. Is there anything I can do for you, Mother?
RHODA. Yes. After I'm cremated, put me with Uncle Hub's ashes. He failed as a gardener, too. All he could ever raise was a glass of beer.
DILLSON. (*Beams.*) Why don't you eat something? I always feel better when I eat something.
RHODA. No, thanks. I've just swallowed my pride. What *could* have happened to that plant?
DILLSON. (*Uneasily.*) I think I'd better be going.
MARIGOLD. Wait, Dillson, come in the kitchen. I want to talk to you.
DILLSON. (*Backs away.*) No—I got to hurry home. I forgot something.
MARIGOLD. (*Scornfully.*) What?
DILLSON. I can't remember. I forgot what I forgot. (*He hurries to escape. He stops at the door.*) Sorry, Mrs. Greenleaf, that it turned out to be a real ickie-sticky-wicket. (*He goes out.*)
MARIGOLD. Mother—there's something I don't know whether or not I ought to tell you.
RHODA. Don't tell me anything unpleasant. Not today. Leave that to Clara. She's better at it than you are.
MARIGOLD. OK. Well, who was it said, "It'll be funny when it stops hurting"?
RHODA. A dentist. Which is about as much wisdom as you'll find in a wisdom tooth.
MARIGOLD. I was just trying. (*Rises and starts for kitchen. She stops and raises one finger.*) Remember—"Tany"!
RHODA. Oh, not games again.
MARIGOLD. That stands for—"There's Always Next Year." (*She goes into kitchen.*)
RHODA. "Tany." It also stands for "Tomorrow, Another Nasty Yowl." (*She pours a drink and raises glass.*) To next year. (*Drinks a little and raises glass.*) To the Titanic. To Napoleon. (*Drinks and lifts glass again.*) To Mary, Queen of Scots. Cheer up, Mary. I lost a greenhouse. You only lost your head. (*Her lips quiver and she puts her head down on her folded arms on the table. The door opens and Vincent comes in. He takes off his coat and tie. He sees his wife apparently asleep. He walks down and trys to peer under her head. She jumps up suddenly and* shrieks *at him.*) You! Don't *speak* to me! *You're* to blame. You! You're to blame, *you!* (*He backs up, startled at her out-*

51

burst. *She pursues him.*) *I didn't want to be President. I just wanted a greenhouse. Like the White House. But you wouldn't give me one. No—you'd rather gamble on a rabbit!* (*He continues to back up, hands before his face as if tc ward off a blow.*) *Look what you've driven me to! Look at me bleeding! Are you happy!* (*He shakes his head frantically, backing to the stairs as she continues to wave her finger under his nose.*) *My Virgin is sick as a dog, Dying! And you made a promise, didn't you? Don't answer. You're saved! Because I went down with the Titanic. Well, what have you got to say for yourself! Don't answer!* (*He flees up the stairs. Rhoda pauses for a moment and then returns to sit by the table.*) *Well, I'm not going to let it upset me. There's always "Tany." All right—I've lost. But I don't care. I don't really care at all.* (*Her face puckers up like that of a frustrated baby and she begins to bawl loudly in the same manner.*)

CURTAIN

ACT THREE

SCENE 2

PLACE: *The same.*
TIME: *A couple of hours later.*
AT RISE: *Rhoda stands alone behind the card table* U. *She takes a gulp from her glass and then hammers on the table with the gavel for the attention of no one.*

RHODA. (*Slurs slightly.*) The sixth-hundred meeting of the Upper South Ho-Ho-Kus Little Lake Garden Club will now come to order. See-vous-play. (*She starts to sing alone.*)
"OH, GIRLS OF THE GARDEN CLUB ARE WE
WHEN FLOWERS DIE
WE STOP TO CRY
IT'S SUCH A SOLEMN CALAMITY
WE'RE SOAKING WET
WITH HUMAN SWEAT
WE'RE NOT AS SWEET AS WE'D LIKE TO BE" (*She stops to drain her glass, only to find it empty. She weaves* D. *only to find the bottle empty. She shakes it upside down for the last drop, to no avail. She*

looks up at hanging plant.) Oh, shut up! (*She climbs up on her small watering ladder and sings again.*)
"OOOOH—GIRLS OF THE GARDEN CLUB ARE WE
AND LILLYBELLE
CAN GO TO HELL
SHE'S GOT A STING LIKE A BUMBLE BEE.
(*She throws her head back like a yowling dog.*)
OOOOOH—"
(*The front door opens and Dillson enters.*)
DILLSON. Can I see you, Mrs. Greenleaf?
RHODA. Unless you're blind.
DILLSON. My conscience has been bothering me and I have a confession to make.
RHODA. See the Pope. Go home and eat something. Your father—your crab grass—an old sock—
DILLSON. Are you all right, Mrs. Greenleaf?
RHODA. Of course I'm all right. And don't ask what I'm doing up here.
DILLSON. I can see. You're higher than a kite. (*Calls upstairs.*) Marigold! (*Turns back to Rhoda.*) You shouldn't ought to let a little thing like a sick plant get ya down, Mrs. Greenleaf. (*Smiles smugly.*) Think of all the sick *people* in the world.
RHODA. (*Steps down and puts her hands on Dillson's shoulder.*) Dillson, my boy, in terms of the life span of mice, you're about six thousand, eight hundred and thirteen years old. But there's something you haven't learned. So I'm going to enlighten you because I'm fifty thousand and twenty-two years old—as a mouse. And it's this—comparing my misery to the misery of others has never yet made me feel better. And reading the obituaries has never made me feel lucky. It only reminds me that I could be next. So put that in your little rat brain and file it.
DILLSON. Boy—you really are pissed. (*Calls upstairs.*) Marigold!
MARIGOLD. (*Comes downstairs.*) Oh, it's you again. Mister Genius.
DILLSON. Marigold—I think your mother is stinko.
RHODA. That's perfectly correct. S—T—I—N—K—O. "Shipwrecked—thwarted—ignored—neutered and knocked out."
MARIGOLD. Mother—do you want some coffee?
RHODA. No. Just a greenhouse where I could raise Vincent's taxes. (*She puts her arms around both of them.*) My dear little fertile mice, don't ever join a Garden Club. Join the Foreign Legion—

join the Mafia. But not a Garden Club. You'll just have your heart broken by a Sleeping Virgin or a Migratory Yehudi.
DILLSON. *(Looks at Marigold.)* Crocked!
RHODA. Not crocked. Cracked.
DILLSON. Well, that's what I wanted to explain to you, Mrs. Greenleaf. About what really happened to your Sleeping Virgin.
RHODA. That's very kind of you, Dillson—to try and cheer me up. But it's not your responsibility, dear boy.
DILLSON. But you're wrong, Mrs. Greenleaf.
RHODA. Yes—my grammar. "Try *to*" not "try and." But I don't really feel all that badly about losing. Because I've got something no one can ever take away from me. My plant talked to me. I'll have that memory as long as I live.
DILLSON. *(Stares at her a moment undecided, and then turns to Marigold.)* What do I say?
MARIGOLD. Your prayers. You're lucky. *(To her mother.)* Mother—don't you want to lie down?
RHODA. Yes. In my grave.
MARIGOLD. We'll take you up to your room; you'll feel better. *(They help with each on one side of her.)*
DILLSON. Maybe if she took a swim?
RHODA. I've just done that. I dove into an empty pool.
DILLSON. When my Dad comes home like this, Mom throws cold water in his face.
RHODA. I've just had that done to me, too. By Lillybelle. Oui-oui! *(As they are halfway up the stairs the door bursts open and Evie and Dora race* D.*)*
EVIE. *(Calls.)* Rhoda! Rhoda! Where are you? *(Turns to Dora in alarm.)* We're too late! She's killed herself!
RHODA. Here I am—halfway to heaven.
EVIE. Come down, quick! We've something very odd to tell you.
DORA. Very odd.
RHODA. Well, odds are it won't be very good. *(Starts back down.)* Why aren't you two at the Flower Show—with the other daffodils?
EVIE. We were but Cora sent us back to get you. Something amazing has happened.
DORA. Amazing.
EVIE. You won't believe it! I was there and I still can't believe it.
DORA. Me neither.
RHODA. *(Grabs her.)* It spoke before it died!
EVIE. Who?

54

DORA. Who?
EVIE. Who died?
DORA. Who died?
RHODA. My poor sick little Virgin.
EVIE. It didn't die. It suddenly began growing! Right before your eyes. It was like—like being in Disneyland.
DORA. That's in Florida.
EVIE. It's grown two feet in less than two hours.
DORA. Less.
EVIE. And the blossoms! They grew twice as big, too.
DORA. Twice.
EVIE. And their fragrance was just overpowering. Like—like rare old wine. Intoxicating.
DORA. Intoxicating.
EVIE. People crowded around and began applauding! It was a kind of botanical miracle. One woman fell to her knees and began praying.
DORA. Puerto Rican.
RHODA. You know the trouble with you two girls? You drink before noon.
EVIE. It's true. Come and see.
DORA. With us.
MARIGOLD. Mother—why should they lie?
RHODA. It really—revived?
EVIE. Cross my heart and hope to die.
DORA. Me, too.
RHODA. Did it—did it win first prize?
EVIE. We don't know. You see there was a dispute. Lillybelle got hold of the judge and demanded an investigation. She claims it was all a trick.
DORA. That's what she claimed.
RHODA. How could it be a trick!
DORA. I don't know. With wires or something. Or drugged. Race horses are.
DORA. Drugged.
RHODA. My Virgin isn't a horse! What did the judge decide?
EVIE. We don't know. I told you—we left.
DORA. She told you.
RHODA. Then it didn't win?
EVIE. Well, it didn't *didn't.*
DORA. Didn't didn't.

RHODA. I've got to know. Did it or didn't it!
EVIE. I told you—it didn't didn't and didn't did.
DORA. Didn't didn't and didn't did.
RHODA. I'm going to the Flower Show! Dillson, get me your motorbike. (*Before he can answer, the front door flys open and the entire Garden Club, with the exception of Cora, Birdie and Clara, pour into the room, clamoring.*)
ALL.
You won, Rhoda!
Congratulations!
You should have been there.
You won hands down.
It was wonderful.
You've never seen anything like it!
They cheered.
You'll be in the papers.
We're so proud of you.
You've made history, Rhoda.
You should have been there.
You made history, dear.
(*The clamor subsides. Rhoda gulps.*)
RHODA. I—I won?
THELMA. You won.
RHODA. Then I'm President?
AGNES. Madam President.
MARGARET. Best man wins.
RITA. Best gardener.
TRUDI. Tell us the secret, Rhoda. What do you give it?
RHODA. Love. Just love.
BERTHA. Well, you've put Upper South Ho-ho-kus Little Lake on the map.
RHODA. Tell me—what did Lillybelle say when it was announced.
LORRAINE. Nothing. But her face fell.
VI. She'll have to have it lifted again.
BESSIE. (*At the window.*) Girls! Girls! Clara, Cora and Birdie are coming in with the winning plant now.
LORRAINE. Now, you see for yourself. (*They wait. The door opens and Cora, followed by Clara and Birdie enter carrying the plant. It is enormous. [Duplicate] And its blossoms have grown to a fantastic size. It is placed Center Stage where they all gather around it in awe.*)

DILLSON. Boy o' boy! Look at her! That's one Sleeping Virgin that sure woke up with a bang.
BIRDIE. That's how all virgins wake up, Dillson.
DEDE. Birdie! Not in front of Dillson—he's only a boy.
DILLSON. That's alright, Mrs. Smithers. I got straight A's in Sex Orientation.
RHODA. (*Staring at plant.*) I can't believe it.
EVIE. I told you you wouldn't.
DORA. That's what she told you.
BIRDIE. Shows you what you can do with a dried testicle.
EVIE. We don't know what you did to do it but whatever you did do you did it, didn't she!
DORA. You can say that again.
EVIE. Alright. We don't know what you did to do it but whatever you did do, you did it.
BIRDIE. (*Shouts.*) *What'd she say?* (*Front door opens and Vincent enters. He sees the girls and trys to escape up the stairs.*)
RHODA. Oh, no you don't, Vincent. Come back down here. I've got a surprise for you. (*He starts back.*)
BIRDIE. Whenever a wife tells her husband she's got a surprise for him, he thinks she's pregnant.
CLARA. Not pregnant—just President.
DEDE. She's put the Upper South Ho-Ho-Kus Little Lake Garden Club on the map! Lower North Ho-Ho-Kus will be livid. (*Vincent looks around at the girls.*)
RHODA. You said if I became President you'd give me a greenhouse. But you didn't say President of what.
EVIE. Write her a check, Vincent. If you renege now, you'll be blackballed from Rotary.
DEDE. Blackballed.
RHODA. And you won't win a Rabbit next year. (*Vincent shrugs and sits down to write a check.*) Oh, I'm so happy. I'm going to have a greenhouse big enough to plant a banana tree.
CLARA. You couldn't possibly do that, Rhoda.
RHODA. I could if I wanted to.
CLARA. No, you couldn't. Because a banana isn't a tree. A tree has wood. Horticulturally speaking, a banana is an herb.
BIRDIE. Imagine that! I've been eating herbs all my life thinking they were bananas. (*Vincent rises and hands Rhoda a check.*)
RHODA. Thank you, dear. Don't you want to say something to the girls?

GIRLS. Speech! Speech! Speech! (*Vincent looks around the room, then crosses down to the Sleeping Virgin.*)
RHODA. My husband is a man of very few words. (*Vincent looks at the plant, sticks out his tongue and gives it a loud, wet raspberry. As the girls gasp and cluck, he stalks with head held high into the kitchen.*)
CLARA. Men! All they think about is money, meals and sex.
CORA. In reverse order.
BIRDIE. (*Shouts.*) What'd Vincent say? (*Dede sticks her tongue out and repeats Vincent's raspberry.*) I thought that's what he said.
RHODA. I should have had more faith. That dear plant *told* me it would try to win.
CORA. Oh, Rhoda—you still don't believe it spoke to you, do you?
RHODA. I *heard* it!
CORA. You fool yourself, I've done it. Only last month I was in my kitchen alone when I heard something say— (*Lowers her voice pontifically.*) "This is the voice of an angel from above, Cora Hickenbougthan. I shall put a curse on thee unless—" Well, I nearly jumped out of my skin. My son Dillson had rigged up a microphone in my oven and— (*She stares at the plant. Light dawns.*) Wait a minute! (*She examines the flower stand. Dillson slinks into kitchen. Cora finds the mike and holds it up triumphantly.*) I thought so! (*Turns to kitchen door and calls.*) Dillson! (*She waits.*) Dillson Augustus Hickenbougthan—*you* come back in here! (*She waits.*) All right. I'm going to drag you back in here by your dinkie-stinkie-pinkie. (*She starts after him, but as she reaches the kitchen entrance, the front door opens and Lillybelle enters. They all turn in amazement.*)
LILLYBELLE. Bon jour! Bon jour! Oh, how fortunate to find all you girls here. Bon jour!
CLARA. Well, you seem mighty happy for someone who's just lost an election.
LILLYBELLE. Oh, I'm not so sure that's the case. I've just come from the Board of Directors of the Flower Show and there just might have been a teensy-weansy mistake.
RHODA. What do you mean?
LILLYBELLE. Well, Rhoda dear. I had them look up their bylaws. It seems that if a plant is over four feet it can *not* be entered as a flower.
BIRDIE. What's it entered as—a banana?
LILLYBELLE. It comes under the category of a bush or tree. So you just may have to default, Rhoda, "Mon chéri."
CORA. But the judges decided!

LILLYBELLE. Judges can be wrong, then decisions are often reversed. I told those dear directors I'd come over and measure Rhoda's Virgin for them. (*She takes out a tape measure.*)
CORA. You mean she'll have to give her first prize back?
LILLYBELLE. I don't make laws—I just abide by them. Now—if you'll just excuse me, "s'il vou plaît." (*She starts for the plant. When she reaches out—it speaks.*)
PLANT. Get away from me.
LILLYBELLE. (*Turns to Rhoda.*) What did you say?
RHODA. I didn't say anything.
EVIE. Eeek! (*Points.*) The plant! It spoke!
DORA. It spoke!
LILLYBELLE. Don't be silly. Plants can't speak. Did you hear it, Clara?
CLARA. I'm tone deaf. I just grow parsley.
LILLYBELLE. *You* didn't hear it speak, did you, Birdie?
BIRDIE. Oh, "oui, oui."
LILLYBELLE. Well, we'll just see about that. (*To plant.*) If you can speak—say something.
PLANT. Drop dead.
LILLYBELLE. It spoke!
CORA. (*Drops to her knees—overacting a bit.*) A miracle! (*She makes the sign of the cross.*)
BIRDIE. I didn't know you were Puerto Rican, Cora.
LILLYBELLE. It spoke. You all heard it.
PLANT. You come near me and I'll put a curse on you.
LILLYBELLE. A curse?
EVIE. (*Squeals.*) *The Curse of Pomona!*
DORA. A Greek fruit.
LILLYBELLE. It's hostile! I'm afraid to measure it.
BIRDIE. You should be. There's a plant in Africa that eats rats.
PLANT. Go home, Lillybelle Lamont. Go home before I curse thee henceforth.
LILLYBELLE. I'm going mad. I'm going stark raving mad. Nothing is worth this. I don't want to be President. I just want to get out of here. "C'est fini. Fini! Fini!" (*She races out. There is general chatter and laughter.*)
RHODA. Oh, girls—you were wonderful. Especially you, Cora, praying like that. How can I thank you?
CORA. Start praying for *me*. I hurt my knee.
DILLSON. (*Comes out from the kitchen to stand beside his mother.*) Hey—that was a real Fini-fini-funny.

CORA. (*Puts her arm around him proudly.*) Does everyone know my son—Dillson Thomas Edison Hickenbougthan?
DEDE. Isn't it *amazing* how it all worked out? I thought it was a lost cause.
EVIE. You must feel wonderful, Rhoda.
DORA. Wonderful!
RHODA. I do. I feel like flying. Like singing. (*She starts to sing.*)
OH, GIRLS OF THE GARDEN CLUB ARE WE
(*The others join in one by one.*)
ALL.
OUR WORK CONFIRMS
WE'RE FRIENDS OF WORMS
WE DIG IN THE NAME OF BOT-TAN-EE
(*The curtain starts to descend slowly as all sing loudly as a chorus.*)
MEN WON'T DO IT
THEY POOH-POOH IT
OH, GIRLS OF THE GARDEN CLUB ARE WE
ARE WE—
ARE WE—
WE *ARE!*
BIRDIE. (*Rises and crosses stage.*) I'm getting the hell out of here. You girls are a bunch of goddam nuts. (*They all begin to cluck loudly—a penfull of indignant chickens.*)

CURTAIN

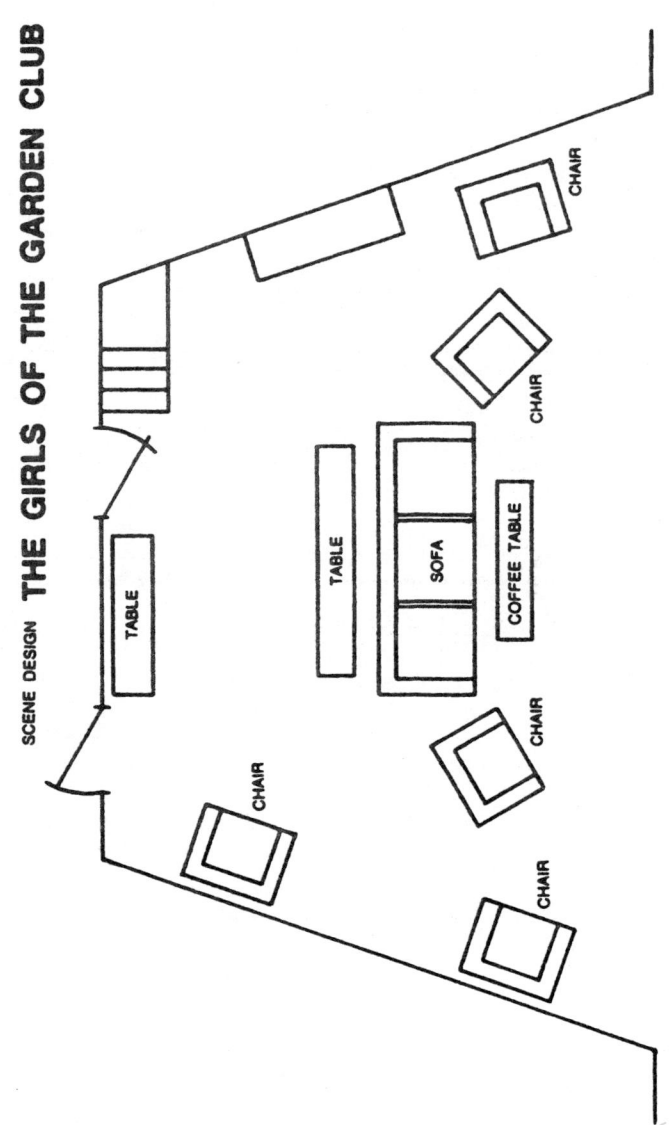

PROPERTY LIST

ACT ONE

Many potted plants
Door chimes
Telephone
Ladder
Books
Watering can
Flower stands
Newspaper
Card table
Snapshot (Rhoda)
Plant bulbs
Coffee urn and cups
Cigarettes and lighter
Cereal bowl and spoon
Beer cans
Horn-rimmed glasses
Umbrella
Bracelets
Wristwatch (Vincent)
Watch (Clara)

ACT TWO

Many chairs
Gavel
Water pitcher and glass
Books and magazines
Table bell
Tray and platters
Potted plant
Key-note whistle
Beer can
Cranberry juice
Plant bulbs
Footstool
Program

ACT THREE
Scene 1

"Sleeping Virgin" plants
Spray gun
Shoe box
Microphone and wire
Wine decanter and glass
Purse
Watering can

ACT THREE
Scene 2

Revived "Virgin" plant
Checkbook
Pen
Tape measure
Decanter and glass
Gavel

NEW PLAYS

★ **YELLOW FACE by David Henry Hwang.** Asian-American playwright DHH leads a protest against the casting of Jonathan Pryce as the Eurasian pimp in the original Broadway production of *Miss Saigon*, condemning the practice as "yellowface." The lines between truth and fiction blur with hilarious and moving results in this unreliable memoir. "A pungent play of ideas with a big heart." –*Variety*. "Fabulously inventive." –*The New Yorker*. [5M, 2W] ISBN: 978-0-8222-2301-6

★ **33 VARIATIONS by Moisés Kaufmann.** A mother coming to terms with her daughter. A composer coming to terms with his genius. And, even though they're separated by 200 years, these two people share an obsession that might, even just for a moment, make time stand still. "A compellingly original and thoroughly watchable play for today." –*Talkin' Broadway*. [4M, 4W] ISBN: 978-0-8222-2392-4

★ **BOOM by Peter Sinn Nachtrieb.** A grad student's online personal ad lures a mysterious journalism student to his subterranean research lab. But when a major catastrophic event strikes the planet, their date takes on evolutionary significance and the fate of humanity hangs in the balance. "Darkly funny dialogue." –*NY Times*. "Literate, coarse, thoughtful, sweet, scabrously inappropriate." –*Washington City Paper*. [1M, 2W] ISBN: 978-0-8222-2370-2

★ **LOVE, LOSS AND WHAT I WORE by Nora Ephron and Delia Ephron, based on the book by Ilene Beckerman.** A play of monologues and ensemble pieces about women, clothes and memory covering all the important subjects—mothers, prom dresses, mothers, buying bras, mothers, hating purses and why we only wear black. "Funny, compelling." –*NY Times*. "So funny and so powerful." –*WowOwow.com*. [5W] ISBN: 978-0-8222-2355-9

★ **CIRCLE MIRROR TRANSFORMATION by Annie Baker.** When four lost New Englanders enrolled in Marty's community center drama class experiment with harmless games, hearts are quietly torn apart, and tiny wars of epic proportions are waged and won. "Absorbing, unblinking and sharply funny." –*NY Times*. [2M, 3W] ISBN: 978-0-8222-2445-7

★ **BROKE-OLOGY by Nathan Louis Jackson.** The King family has weathered the hardships of life and survived with their love for each other intact. But when two brothers are called home to take care of their father, they find themselves strangely at odds. "Engaging dialogue." –*TheaterMania.com*. "Assured, bighearted." –*Time Out*. [3M, 1W] ISBN: 978-0-8222-2428-0

DRAMATISTS PLAY SERVICE, INC.
440 Park Avenue South, New York, NY 10016 212-683-8960 Fax 212-213-1539
postmaster@dramatists.com   www.dramatists.com

NEW PLAYS

★ **A CIVIL WAR CHRISTMAS: AN AMERICAN MUSICAL CELEBRATION by Paula Vogel, music by Daryl Waters.** It's 1864, and Washington, D.C. is settling down to the coldest Christmas Eve in years. Intertwining many lives, this musical shows us that the gladness of one's heart is the best gift of all. "Boldly inventive theater, warm and affecting." –*Talkin' Broadway.* "Crisp strokes of dialogue." –*NY Times.* [12M, 5W] ISBN: 978-0-8222-2361-0

★ **SPEECH & DEBATE by Stephen Karam.** Three teenage misfits in Salem, Oregon discover they are linked by a sex scandal that's rocked their town. "Savvy comedy." –*Variety.* "Hilarious, cliché-free, and immensely entertaining." –*NY Times.* "A strong, rangy play." –*NY Newsday.* [2M, 2W] ISBN: 978-0-8222-2286-6

★ **DIVIDING THE ESTATE by Horton Foote.** Matriarch Stella Gordon is determined not to divide her 100-year-old Texas estate, despite her family's declining wealth and the looming financial crisis. But her three children have another plan. "Goes for laughs and succeeds." –*NY Daily News.* "The theatrical equivalent of a page-turner." –*Bloomberg.com.* [4M, 9W] ISBN: 978-0-8222-2398-6

★ **WHY TORTURE IS WRONG, AND THE PEOPLE WHO LOVE THEM by Christopher Durang.** Christopher Durang turns political humor upside down with this raucous and provocative satire about America's growing homeland "insecurity." "A smashing new play." –*NY Observer.* "You may laugh yourself silly." –*Bloomberg News.* [4M, 3W] ISBN: 978-0-8222-2401-3

★ **FIFTY WORDS by Michael Weller.** While their nine-year-old son is away for the night on his first sleepover, Adam and Jan have an evening alone together, beginning a suspenseful nightlong roller-coaster ride of revelation, rancor, passion and humor. "Mr. Weller is a bold and productive dramatist." –*NY Times.* [1M, 1W] ISBN: 978-0-8222-2348-1

★ **BECKY'S NEW CAR by Steven Dietz.** Becky Foster is caught in middle age, middle management and in a middling marriage—with no prospects for change on the horizon. Then one night a socially inept and grief-struck millionaire stumbles into the car dealership where Becky works. "Gently and consistently funny." –*Variety.* "Perfect blend of hilarious comedy and substantial weight." –*Broadway Hour.* [4M, 3W] ISBN: 978-0-8222-2393-1

DRAMATISTS PLAY SERVICE, INC.
440 Park Avenue South, New York, NY 10016 212-683-8960 Fax 212-213-1539
postmaster@dramatists.com   www.dramatists.com

NEW PLAYS

★ **AT HOME AT THE ZOO by Edward Albee.** Edward Albee delves deeper into his play THE ZOO STORY by adding a first act, HOMELIFE, which precedes Peter's fateful meeting with Jerry on a park bench in Central Park. "An essential and heartening experience." –*NY Times.* "Darkly comic and thrilling." –*Time Out.* "Genuinely fascinating." –*Journal News.* [2M, 1W] ISBN: 978-0-8222-2317-7

★ **PASSING STRANGE book and lyrics by Stew, music by Stew and Heidi Rodewald, created in collaboration with Annie Dorsen.** A daring musical about a young bohemian that takes you from black middle-class America to Amsterdam, Berlin and beyond on a journey towards personal and artistic authenticity. "Fresh, exuberant, bracingly inventive, bitingly funny, and full of heart." –*NY Times.* "The freshest musical in town!" –*Wall Street Journal.* "Excellent songs and a vulnerable heart." –*Variety.* [4M, 3W] ISBN: 978-0-8222-2400-6

★ **REASONS TO BE PRETTY by Neil LaBute.** Greg really, truly adores his girlfriend, Steph. Unfortunately, he also thinks she has a few physical imperfections, and when he mentions them, all hell breaks loose. "Tight, tense and emotionally true." –*Time Magazine.* "Lively and compulsively watchable." –*The Record.* [2M, 2W] ISBN: 978-0-8222-2394-8

★ **OPUS by Michael Hollinger.** With only a few days to rehearse a grueling Beethoven masterpiece, a world-class string quartet struggles to prepare their highest-profile performance ever—a televised ceremony at the White House. "Intimate, intense and profoundly moving." –*Time Out.* "Worthy of scores of bravissimos." –*BroadwayWorld.com.* [4M, 1W] ISBN: 978-0-8222-2363-4

★ **BECKY SHAW by Gina Gionfriddo.** When an evening calculated to bring happiness takes a dark turn, crisis and comedy ensue in this wickedly funny play that asks what we owe the people we love and the strangers who land on our doorstep. "As engrossing as it is ferociously funny." –*NY Times.* "Gionfriddo is some kind of genius." –*Variety.* [2M, 3W] ISBN: 978-0-8222-2402-0

★ **KICKING A DEAD HORSE by Sam Shepard.** Hobart Struther's horse has just dropped dead. In an eighty-minute monologue, he discusses what path brought him here in the first place, the fate of his marriage, his career, politics and eventually the nature of the universe. "Deeply instinctual and intuitive." –*NY Times.* "The brilliance is in the infinite reverberations Shepard extracts from his simple metaphor." –*TheaterMania.* [1M, 1W] ISBN: 978-0-8222-2336-8

DRAMATISTS PLAY SERVICE, INC.
440 Park Avenue South, New York, NY 10016   212-683-8960   Fax 212-213-1539
postmaster@dramatists.com   www.dramatists.com

NEW PLAYS

★ **AUGUST: OSAGE COUNTY by Tracy Letts.** WINNER OF THE 2008 PULITZER PRIZE AND TONY AWARD. When the large Weston family reunites after Dad disappears, their Oklahoma homestead explodes in a maelstrom of repressed truths and unsettling secrets. "Fiercely funny and bitingly sad." –*NY Times.* "Ferociously entertaining." –*Variety.* "A hugely ambitious, highly combustible saga." –*NY Daily News.* [6M, 7W] ISBN: 978-0-8222-2300-9

★ **RUINED by Lynn Nottage.** WINNER OF THE 2009 PULITZER PRIZE. Set in a small mining town in Democratic Republic of Congo, RUINED is a haunting, probing work about the resilience of the human spirit during times of war. "A full-immersion drama of shocking complexity and moral ambiguity." –*Variety.* "Sincere, passionate, courageous." –*Chicago Tribune.* [8M, 4W] ISBN: 978-0-8222-2390-0

★ **GOD OF CARNAGE by Yasmina Reza, translated by Christopher Hampton.** WINNER OF THE 2009 TONY AWARD. A playground altercation between boys brings together their Brooklyn parents, leaving the couples in tatters as the rum flows and tensions explode. "Satisfyingly primitive entertainment." –*NY Times.* "Elegant, acerbic, entertainingly fueled on pure bile." –*Variety.* [2M, 2W] ISBN: 978-0-8222-2399-3

★ **THE SEAFARER by Conor McPherson.** Sharky has returned to Dublin to look after his irascible, aging brother. Old drinking buddies Ivan and Nicky are holed up at the house too, hoping to play some cards. But with the arrival of a stranger from the distant past, the stakes are raised ever higher. "Dark and enthralling Christmas fable." –*NY Times.* "A timeless classic." –*Hollywood Reporter.* [5M] ISBN: 978-0-8222-2284-2

★ **THE NEW CENTURY by Paul Rudnick.** When the playwright is Paul Rudnick, expectations are geared for a play both hilarious and smart, and this provocative and outrageous comedy is no exception. "The one-liners fly like rockets." –*NY Times.* "The funniest playwright around." –*Journal News.* [2M, 3W] ISBN: 978-0-8222-2315-3

★ **SHIPWRECKED! AN ENTERTAINMENT—THE AMAZING ADVENTURES OF LOUIS DE ROUGEMONT (AS TOLD BY HIMSELF) by Donald Margulies.** The amazing story of bravery, survival and celebrity that left nineteenth-century England spellbound. Dare to be whisked away. "A deft, literate narrative." –*LA Times.* "Springs to life like a theatrical pop-up book." –*NY Times.* [2M, 1W] ISBN: 978-0-8222-2341-2

DRAMATISTS PLAY SERVICE, INC.
440 Park Avenue South, New York, NY 10016   212-683-8960   Fax 212-213-1539
postmaster@dramatists.com   www.dramatists.com